INNOVATIVE RESTAURANT INTERIORS | INTÉRIEURS INNOVANTS DE RESTAURANTS | NUEVO DISEÑO DE RESTAURANTES | ARREDAMENTI INNOVATIVI PER RISTORANTI

TASTE IT!

promopress

TASTE IT!

INNOVATIVE RESTAURANT INTERIORS
INTÉRIEURS INNOVANTS DE RESTAURANTS
NUEVO DISEÑO DE RESTAURANTES
ARREDAMENTI INNOVATIVI PER RISTORANTI

Translators of the preface:
English / French / Spanish / Italian translator: Satèl·lit bcn - Hugo Steckelmacher / Olivier Gilbert / Vanesa Hernández / Daniel Frisano-Paulon

PROMOPRESS is a commercial brand of:
Promotora de Prensa Internacional S.A.
C/ Ausiàs March, 124
08013 Barcelona, Spain
Phone: +34 93 245 14 64
Fax: +34 93 265 48 83
info@promopress.es
www.promopress.es
www.promopresseditions.com

Sponsored by Design 360°
– Concept and Design Magazine

Edited and produced by
Sandu Publishing Co., Ltd.

Book design, concepts & art direction by
Sandu Publishing Co., Ltd.

sandu.publishing@gmail.com
www.sandupublishing.com

Cover project by ILMIODESIGN

ISBN 978-84-92810-58-1

Printed in China

PREFACE

by Antonio Di Oronzo

Antonio Di Oronzo, principal
bluarch architecture + interiors + lighting
professor of architecture [City College of New York – Spitzer School of Architecture]

Restaurants are the ultimate experiential venues. They offer multi-sensorial narratives of flavors and smells, including a sight of what is about to be tasted [inherently a sub-narrative of anticipation], the mediated touch of what is being cut, rolled, scooped via a utensil and, all around, the sound of dishes and utensils, glasses of good wine and convivial chatter. Beyond the private sphere of the sensorial experience of the food, there is the public narrative of the meal, often shared with people who are significant to us... the flavors layered with laughter, a bite is the threshold to a romantic moment, and a sip crowns a celebration.

These are the premises for the process of designing a restaurant. The architect and the designer are tasked with defining the spatial realm of this sequence of sensorial moments, and they do so with different approaches, attitudes and aptitudes. They always, however, set out with the intent of complementing and/or enriching the uniquely intimate experience of consuming food with the public rite of consuming the diners within the space.

A newfound appreciation for food has emerged which is permeating every level of the culinary spectrum and influencing the interiors and architecture of eateries around the globe. There are varied attitudes toward food designed to cater to a specific clientele, whether it is sophisticated up-market or back-to-basics. Furthermore, the continual proliferation of these establishments has compelled owners to offer evermore unique design values, which are used as a source of distinction and identity. Architects and designers have seized this opportunity to create spaces which are formally, technically, and technologically at the forefront of architectural innovation and research.

The projects in the following pages portend an ever-evolving scenario of exciting developments. This book is an indispensable compendium of outstanding restaurant venues from across the globe. It showcases remarkable speculative reach and technological advancements which deliver extraordinary formal and experiential values.

The English say, "spread the table and contention will cease". Enjoy this parade of extraordinary venues where visitors quench, sate, and ultimately find happiness.

PRÉFACE

by Antonio Di Oronzo

Antonio Di Oronzo, Directeur
bluarch architecture + interiors + lighting
Professeur d'Architecture [City College of New York – Bernard and Anne Spitzer School of Architecture]

Les restaurants sont devenus des lieux d'expériences nouvelles. Ils offrent un voyage à travers toute la gamme des sens : les saveurs et les odeurs auxquels s'ajoutent la vue de ce qui est sur le point de se déguster [nous plongeant ainsi dans une attente délicieuse], le touché de ce qui est coupé, enroulé ou modelé à l'aide d'un ustensile et, autour de nous, une atmosphère sonore teintée des bruits de couverts et de vaisselles, des verres de bon vin et des discussions conviviales. Mais au-delà d'une expérience sensorielle il y a le caractère public du repas, souvent partagés avec des gens qui nous importent ... des saveurs s'entremêlent aux rires, une bouchée sous-tend un moment romantique et une gorgée couronne une célébration.

Ceux sont les principes qui régissent le processus de création d'un restaurant que nous allons découvrir. L'architecte et le designer sont chargés de définir le contexte spatial de cette séquence de moments sensoriels, et ils le font avec des approches, des attitudes et des aptitudes différentes. Ils ont cependant toujours à l'esprit l'intention de compléter et / ou d'enrichir l'expérience unique et intime de savourer une cuisine dans le respect d'un rite publique qui implique un certain espace.

Récemment, une nouvelle façon de vivre la cuisine dans toutes ses diversités culinaires a émergé et a, sans aucun doute, influencé le design d'intérieur et l'architecture des espaces de restauration à travers le monde. Il existe différentes manières d'aborder la gastronomie afin de répondre à une clientèle spécifique, qu'elle soit sophistiquée ou haut de gamme ou plus conventionnelle. En outre, le foisonnement de ces établissements a contraint les propriétaires à se démarquer en faisant appel à un design d'intérieur toujours plus exclusif. Architectes et designers ont saisi cette opportunité pour créer des espaces qui sont formellement, techniquement et technologiquement à la pointe de l'innovation et recherche architecturale.

Les projets dans les pages qui suivent laissent présager un scénario en constante évolution caractérisé par des développements passionnants. Ce livre est un recueil indispensable des restaurants à connaitre à travers le globe. Il met en valeur les ressorts spéculatifs remarquables et les avancées technologiques qui offrent d'extraordinaires qualités formelles et empiriques.

Les Anglais ont coutume de dire «mettons la table et les tensions se dissiperont" Nous vous invitons à profiter de ces endroits extraordinaires où les visiteurs cherchent à satisfaire leur curiosité et finalement trouver le bonheur.

PREFACIO

by Antonio Di Oronzo

Antonio Di Oronzo, Director
bluarch architecture + interiors + lighting
Profesor de Arquitectura (City College de Nueva York, Bernard and Anne Spitzer School of Architecture)

Los restaurantes se han puesto de moda como escenarios en los que vivir nuevas experiencias. Nos ofrecen todo tipo de aventuras multisensoriales protagonizadas por olores y sabores, incluida la perspectiva visual de aquello que se está a punto de probar [lo que conlleva un cierto componente de anticipación y expectativa] y el tacto de los alimentos cortados, enrollados o servidos; todo ello ambientado por el sonido de los platos y utensilios de cocina, las copas de buen vino y el eco de una charla amable. Más allá del ámbito privado de las experiencias sensoriales vinculadas a la comida, existe también su dimensión pública, puesto que solemos compartirla con personas que son importantes para nosotros. El sonido de las risas matiza cada sabor. Cada bocado es el umbral hacia un momento romántico, y cada sorbo corona la celebración.

A continuación veremos algunos de los principios que rigen el proceso de diseño de un restaurante. El arquitecto y el diseñador son los encargados de definir el espacio en que se desarrollará esta secuencia de momentos sensoriales y, para hacerlo, recurren a diversos enfoques, actitudes y aptitudes. No obstante, su trabajo siempre está presidido por la intención de complementar - o incluso de enriquecer - la experiencia de consumir alimentos con el ritual público que supone hacerlo en un determinado contexto espacial.

Recientemente, ha surgido una nueva forma de disfrutar de la comida que está presente en todos los niveles del espectro culinario y que, sin duda, ha acabado influyendo en la arquitectura y en el diseño interior de los establecimientos de restauración de todo el mundo. Existen numerosas formas de abordar la comida para atraer a una determinada clientela, tanto en los locales sofisticados o de alta categoría como en los más convencionales. Además, la constante proliferación de este tipo de establecimientos ha obligado a los empresarios a ofrecer cada vez más valor añadido, en lo que se refiere a la exclusividad del diseño, como medio de distinción y de identidad. Los arquitectos y diseñadores han aprovechado esta oportunidad para crear espacios que se sitúan formal, técnica y tecnológicamente a la cabeza de la innovación y de la investigación arquitectónica.

Los proyectos que se abordan en las páginas siguientes hacen presagiar un escenario de evolución constante, caracterizado por emocionantes hitos de desarrollo. Este libro es un compendio indispensable de los establecimientos de restauración más notables de todo el mundo. Pone de manifiesto el gran alcance especulativo y los avances tecnológicos que generan extraordinarios valores formales y empíricos. Los ingleses suelen utilizar la expresión "pongamos la mesa para relajar el ambiente". Le invitamos a que disfrute de estos extraordinarios establecimientos en los que los visitantes buscan saciar su curiosidad y donde, finalmente, encuentran la felicidad.

PREFAZIONE

by Antonio Di Oronzo

Antonio Di Oronzo, Titolare
bluarch architecture + interiors + lighting
Professore di Architettura [City College of New York – Bernard and Anne Spitzer School of Architecture]

Il ristorante è la sede estrema per le nostre esperienze: offre narrazioni multisensoriali di sapori e aromi, e per di più un'anteprima visuale di ciò che si sta per gustare [di per sé una sotto-narrazione di avvicinamento], lo stimolo tattile indiretto del materiale tagliato, arrotolato, raccolto con un utensile, il tutto circondato dal suono delle stoviglie e degli utensili, dal tintinnare dei bicchieri di buon vino e dalle conversazioni in compagnia. Oltre la sfera privata dell'esperienza sensoriale del cibo si trova la pubblica narrazione del pasto, sovente condiviso con persone che contano per noi ... sapori ricoperti di risate, un boccone come anticamera a un momento romantico, e un sorso come il coronamento di una celebrazione.

Questi presupposti sono il punto di partenza per il processo del design per un ristorante. L'architetto e il designer sono incaricati di definire il dominio materiale di questa sequenza di momenti sensoriali, e svolgono il loro compito con approcci, atteggiamenti e attitudini diverse, muovendo però in ogni caso dall'intenzione di complementare e/o arricchire l'esperienza unicamente intima del consumo di cibo con il rito pubblico della consumazione dei pasti all'interno dello spazio così creato.

L'apprezzamento per il cibo, ritrovato e riemerso di recente, permea lo spettro culinario a tutti i suoi livelli e influenza l'arredamento e l'architettura dei ristoranti in tutto il mondo. Si riscontrano diversi atteggiamenti nei confronti del cibo, concepiti per rivolgersi a una specifica clientela, si tratti di una nicchia di mercato sofisticata o di un ritorno alle origini. Per di più, la continua proliferazione di questo tipo di locale costringe ormai i titolari a offrire valori di design sempre più unici da usare come fonte di differenziazione e identità. I vari architetti e designer approfittano di queste opportunità per creare spazi formalmente, tecnicamente e tecnologicamente all'avanguardia dell'innovazione e della ricerca architettonica.

I progetti raccolti in queste pagine presagiscono un mutevole scenario fatto di stimolanti sviluppi. Questo libro rappresenta un compendio irrinunciabile di eccezionali locali per la ristorazione provenienti da tutto il mondo e costituisce una vetrina per i notevoli sforzi concettuali e progressi tecnologici che trasmettono straordinari valori formali e d'esperienza.

Un detto inglese dice che "una tavola imbandita mette fine a ogni contesa". Godetevi questa parata di locali straordinari, dove ogni visitatore potrà dissetarsi, saziarsi, e in definitiva trovare la felicità.

CONTENTS

MAZZO Amsterdam Concrete Architectural Associates

Location: Amsterdam, the Netherlands **Floor Area:** 400 sqm **Completion Year:** 2010 **Photography:** Ewout Huibers

The diversity of the fused spaces and the natural restaurant layout need a connecting element: a huge wooden cupboard across the whole restaurant linking all the spaces and organizing them at the same time. The cupboard, created with solid pine wood for storage and display of the products, becomes the stairs to the mezzanine floor, the back bar, point of distribution for the food, the transparent division between the boardroom and restaurant, the wardrobe, the access to the restrooms and the storage for the kids toys.

Five materials determine the ambiance of the raw and honest interior design: power floated concrete, chipped brickwork, stone, pinewood and raw steel. The first three materials are part of the shell of the building; all the new materials are steel and wood.

The window frames in the cupboard and the mezzanine floor in the front of the restaurant are completely made of raw steel. The steel beams and columns are exposed and the extra floor is provided with an untreated expanded metal mesh. The use of honest and simple materials doesn't distract the guests' eye and underlines the fact that the restaurant focuses on the food.

Embracing the past of the building and the name MAZZO by creating a logo that is a controversial, the five letters are made of raw steel and filled with classic amusement lights, referring to the disco days of MAZZO. The light object crowns above the bar and will be noticed even in a flash by the cars and cyclists passing by.

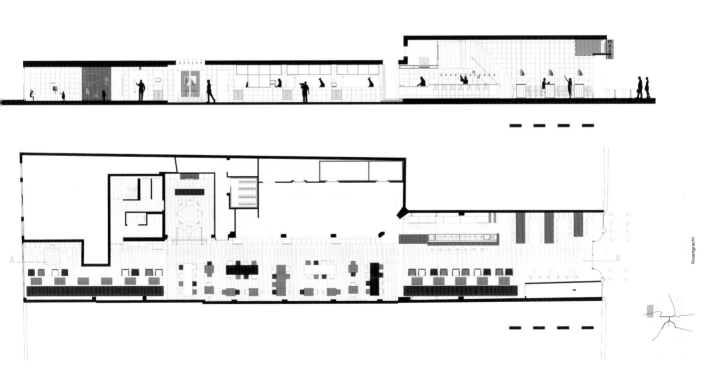

credits tekening MAZZO doorsnede

Restaurant 51 Mut-architecture

Location: Paris, France **Floor Area:** 160 sqm **Completion Year:** 2009 **Photography:** Brigitte Bouillot

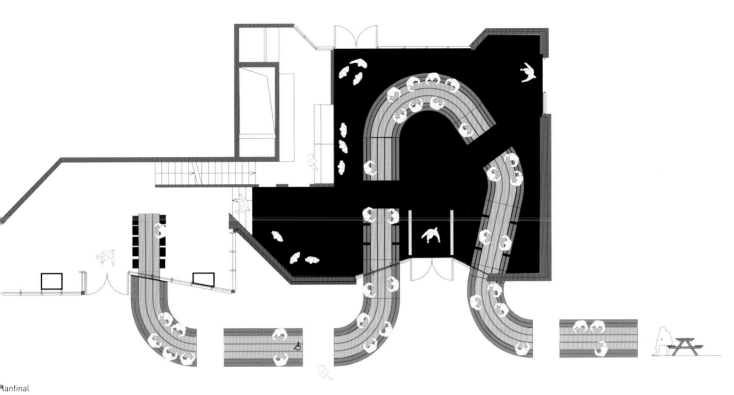

Planfinal

Arriving at the Cinémathèque Française people enter Parc Bercy. When walking into the park the first thing people now see is a picnic table. The table of Restaurant 51 – the restaurant of the Cinematheque - a restaurant designed by Mut-architecture.

They follow the lines of the table, a wooden structure bent and shaped to seat the greatest number of restaurant goers in the most convivial setting. With half the table outdoors, facing Parc Bercy and the other half twisting its path through the interior of the restaurant, people can now sit comfortably close to one another and enjoy a meal or a glass of wine before visiting the Museum, or after leaving it. Like a Lionel toy race car set, the table can be taken apart, fashioned into a number of different variations depending on the needs of the restaurant or changes in the weather.

ATELIER MECANIC Corvin Cristian, Serban Rosca

Location: Bucharest, Romania **Floor Area:** 70 sqm **Completion Year:** 2011 **Photography:** Cosmin Dragomir, Corvin Cristian

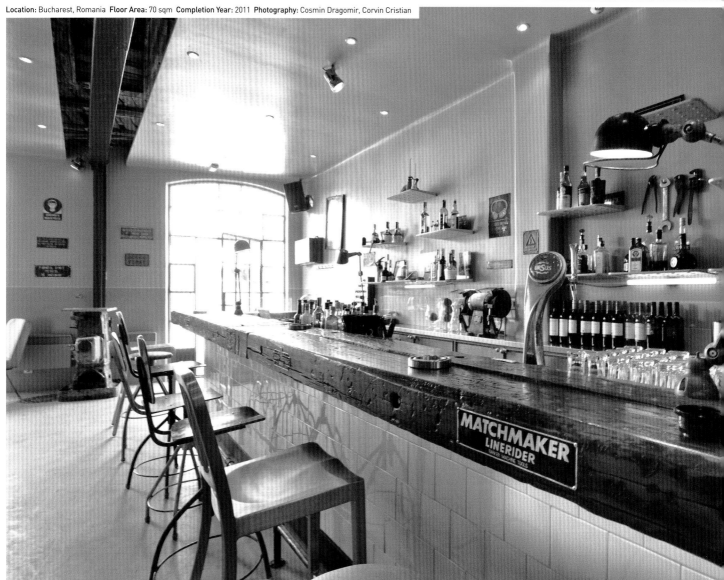

ATELIER MECANIC (Mechanical Workshop) is a bar made of 1950s to 1970s industrial relics, salvaged leftovers, graphics and original furniture. It is a take on the industrialization of the country during communism.

Romanians have an uncomfortable relationship with their past which usually ends up in simply erasing it: factories were perceived as a symbol of communism (which is partly true) and keeping some memories of it was by no means a priority after the Revolution. 50 years of industrialization vanished in no time and is thrown at the scrap yard. ATELIER MECANIC ironically brings them back.

The building is located in the Old Town, a place bustling with bars and clubs. It did not have a history or at least not anymore, whatever remains of what used to be there were gone. Last tenant was another of the few hundreds so called "Irish pubs" popping up in Bucharest at every corner (another curse of globalization).

In the end, it is not that important what used to be there but what could have been. And a mechanical workshop worked just fine because the area used to be populated until recently with small repair shops of all kinds.

PROTEJAȚI-VA
ÎMPOTRIVA TENSIUNILOR
PERICULOASE PRIN
LEGARE LA PAMINT

NU UNGEȚI MAȘINIL
ÎN TIMPUL MERSULUI

CONTROLEAZA CIT MA
DES ETANSEITATEA

RATI NUMAI
CHELARI
ROTECTIE

MU-314

NU REGLAȚI ȘI NU UNGEȚI
MAȘINA ÎN FUNCȚIUNE

WMW

nu fumați decit **IN LOCURILE**
ȘI IN CONDIȚIILE INDICATE
pentru a evita apariția incendiilor.

SCHAUBLIN
Hydropneumatic

POMPA Nr. 1

Central to the philosophy of the café is the imaginary character "Suicide Sue", the enigmatic and fierce former assassin turned restaurateur who adorns the company's walls in the form of paintings, photo projects and lent inspiration to the company's distinctive logo. "Suicide Sue" embodies independence, adventure and kick-ass attitude which is reflected in the design and menu as well as the changing events such as DJs playing on weekends.

Muted colors on the walls, distressed cream colored wooden floorboards and original features such as the detailed cornicing and wooden doorframes set the tone; the large windows towards the street let the light flood in during the day. A large antique Swedish wood burner provides extra warmth throughout the winter months and is the favored hangout place of the owners' dog, Scottie.

Much thought has gone into the interior design which based largely on natural materials and items sourced from all over Europe, such as vintage packing crates, cushions made from recycled military felt blankets, well worn leather armchairs from a former gentleman's club and benches made from reclaimed railway timbers.

Suicide Sue Franziska Stromeyer, Frank Geiger

Location: Berlin, Germany **Floor Area:** 93 sqm **Completion Year:** 2009 **Photography:** Michael Petersohn

Red Pif Restaurant and Wine shop AULÍK FIŠER ARCHITEKTI

Location: Praha, Czech **Floor Area:** 88 sqm **Completion Year:** 2011 **Photography:** AI photography

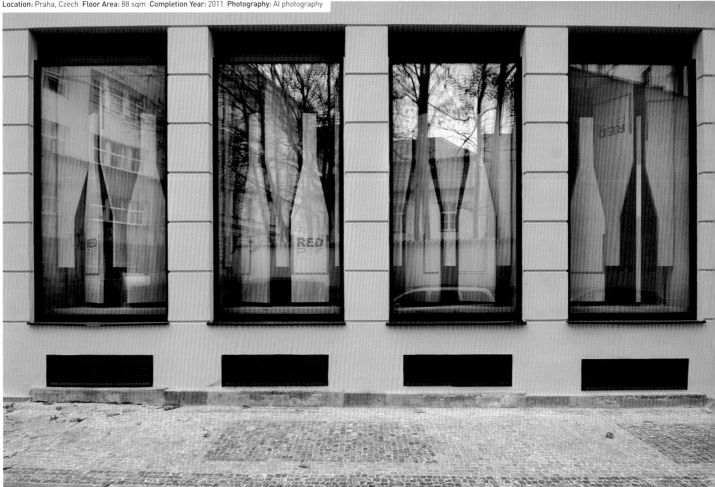

The interior has to be a background allowing the enjoyment of good wine and food here and now. The interior is determined by the high quality of craftsmanship of materials linked to wine producing – oak wood for the floor and bar counter, and reinforcement bars (used in vineyards as supports for vine stems) for bottle shelves. In course of filling the shelves with bottles they disappear from view and transform into a wall of bottles.

When rooms on the ground floor of a house from the 19th century were cleaned of disturbing modifications their authentic quality surfaced again. After the impersonally cool wall paints were removed, the history of the house appeared – remnants of original paints and plasters mingle with scars left after the house was structurally modified.

Touching them and seeing their graphic quality is a special experience. All this is complemented by a painting by Martina Chloupa.

The existing shop windows provide contact with the exterior so important for a restaurant in a city centre. Aulík Fišer Architekti designed rotating screens for evening wine tastings or private celebrations; in their structure a free interpretation of the method of storing bottles in cardboard boxes can be seen. They allow the shop windows to close completely. A visitor then finds himself in a wine cellar separated from the reality of a city. Yet the shop windows do not turn blind, but transform into the restaurant's big logo.

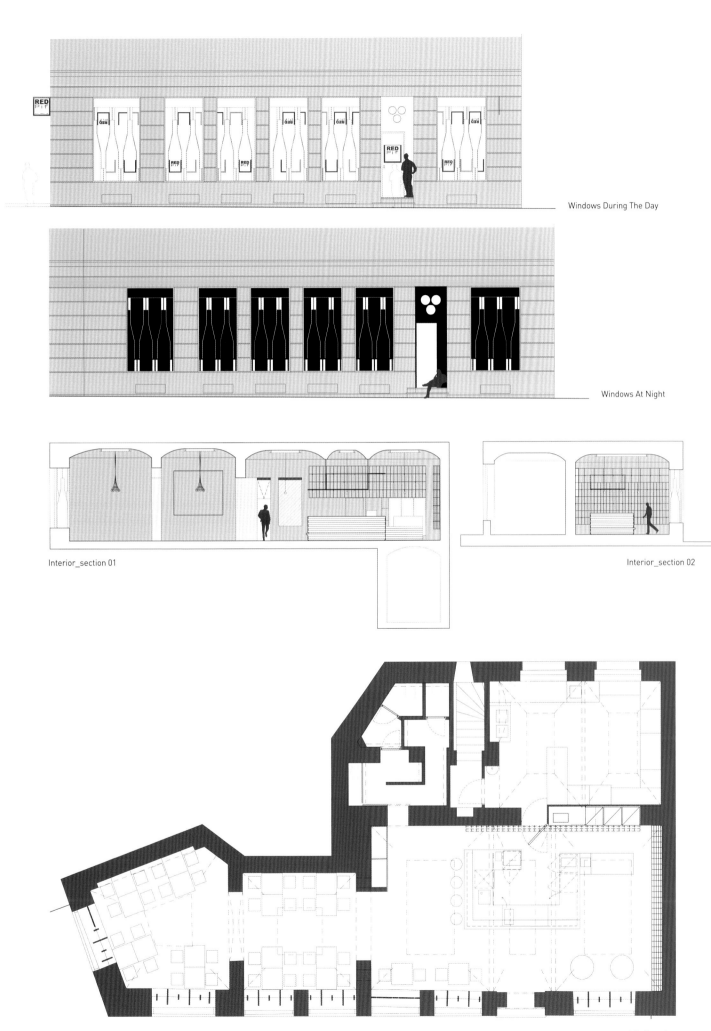

Windows During The Day

Windows At Night

Interior_section 01

Interior_section 02

Interior_plan

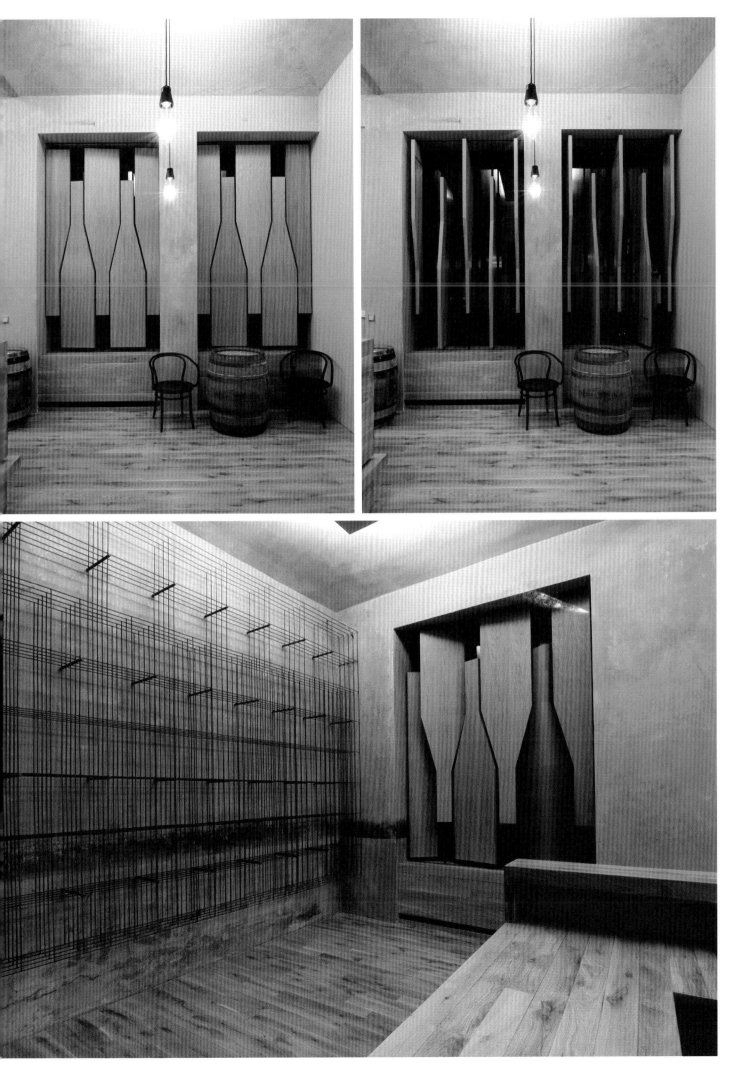

6T7 ESPAI CAFÈ MSB Estudi taller d'arquitectura i disseny

Location: Girona, Spain **Floor Area:** 160 sqm **Completion Year:** 2011 **Photography:** Miquel Merce Arquitecte

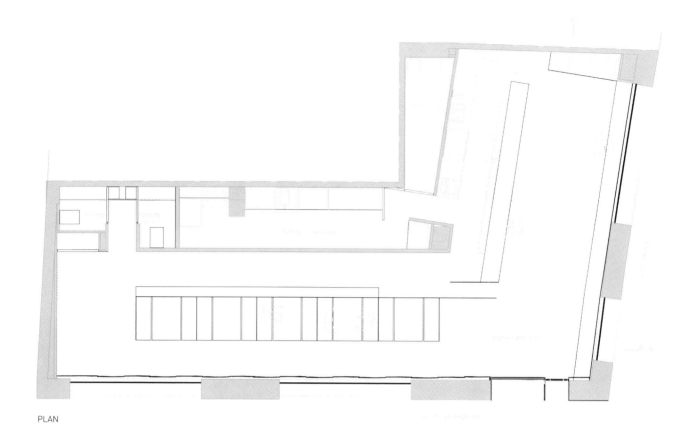

PLAN

6T7 ESPAI CAFÈ is not just a regular cafeteria; it's a meeting place for gatherings and exhibitions. It is located in an alley in the old town, with stony and gray tones. The space was small; the designers optimized it by grouping all elements of the bar, integrated to make the view clean. The entire container is finished with concrete with the same appearance and roughness of the environment. The furniture had to be neutral: they created a piece of furniture to be seen, like a sculpture crafted from steel plate, generating pace and enhancing the shape of the space. The finish is warm and gentle; steel has chosen a dark brown tone and dark streaks that gives a natural texture to it.

In one of the facades facing the street, there is an element, which filters, blurs, and divides the light, a vibrating element that provides texture and roughness to the space, in contrast to the smooth surface of the walls and furniture. It is made by hand in the workshop, composed by frames twisted with steel wire, and hung along the entire wall, making a totally random composition, flexible and filtered. A handmade piece to humanize the space, to get closer and merge the architecture to the people.

Tin Restaurant Bar Berlin karhard architektur + design

Location: Berlin, Germany **Floor Area:** 180 sqm **Completion Year:** 2009 **Photography:** Stefan Wolf Lucks, Joachim Gern

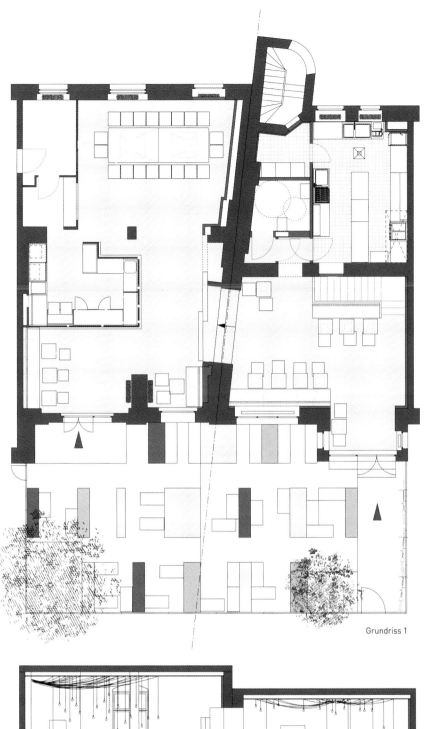

Grundriss 1

At Paul-Lincke Ufer, a popular local and tourist hotspot in Berlin Kreuzberg, a restaurant bar was established from two smaller retail units situated directly on the canal bank. For this new venture, it was necessary to create a kitchen on ground floor level, adequate toilet facilities and a smoking lounge in the basement.

Development of necessary strategic measures is in response to preceding budgetary planning requirements of the scheme. Due to budgetary constraints the design focused on fewer and simpler component materials. The most noticeable characteristic is the lighting which consists of 82 standard halogen bulbs, but which was fitted with specially constructed frames and fasteners.

The main feature of the guest room is the bar. The counter top, a hammered Zinc Plate was hand crafted to create a shimmering surface in contrast to the muted, darker wall and floor surfaces of the space.

Another feature is an exaggerated 4.2m long dining table for 20 people to the rear of the room. The furniture concept was based upon chairs by Konstantin Grcic Myto and manufactured with cement bonded wooden particles by the carpenter.

The interior was decorated in elegant shades of grey in complex coordinated color nuances. The old cast iron radiators were simply cleaned and remain in contrast to the smooth floor.

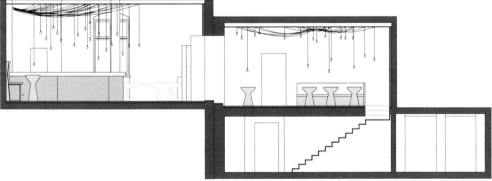

Schnitt a

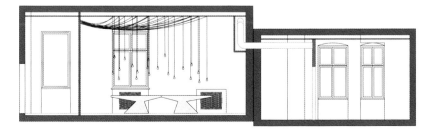

Schnitt b

Ubon Rashed Alfoudari

Location: Kuwait City, Kuwait **Floor Area:** 60 sqm **Completion Year:** 2011/2012 **Photography:** Rashed Alfoudari

Ubon is a Thai bistro located in the core of Kuwait City. It overlooks Fahad Al Salim Street, a street well respected for its commerce back in the days. The space program of this bistro requires an efficient design for all of the kitchen, storage, and toilet areas; allowing for a spacious dining area. For this to be executed, the interior works where to be integrated with the existing structural elements in a harmonious manner.

The Burnt wood panels, infused with the golden copper elements surround the dining area portraying the Asian influence of this bistro. Pendant lights are added to soothe the dining area with their organic shape. Adding to their relevance is the inner golden color they diffuse, a color that has great impact on Thai cultural ornamentation.

A visual continuity is given to the dining area where the wooden grains imprinted on the restroom's concrete walls. The contrast in color and material here is then united by texture. To continue the vertical pattern, the restroom is fitted with a suspended ceiling faucet along with an off-white standalone basin.

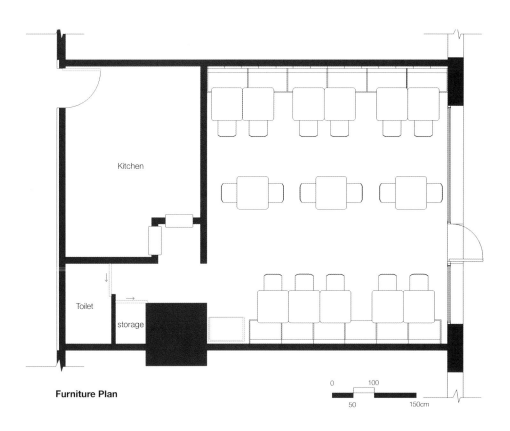

Kitchen

Toilet

storage

Furniture Plan

0   50   100   150cm

Local Italian Gelato

Local Italian Gelato

Local Italian Gelato

DRI DRI_St Martins Lane elips design

Location: London, UK **Floor Area:** 45 sqm **Completion Year:** 2011 **Photography:** Carlo Carossio

The Front Room of St Martins Lane's hotel is a dynamic retail space. It has housed various creative collaborations with partners including The Convenience Store (fashion boutique), Wallpaper (photography exhibition), Angela Hill (vintage books), The Design Museum (film screening) and Nowness (video installation). This time it will be converted by elips design into an idyllic Italian beach, completed with traditional decking, colored beach cabins, sun umbrellas, chairs and tables. The customers will be transported to the Mediterranean in the heart of London's bustling centre enjoying their gelato DRI DRI.

The beach cabins are thought in the way to divide the space and seperate the a back of the house for storage.

The sun umbrellas are wall stickers to create more perspective in a bidimensional space.

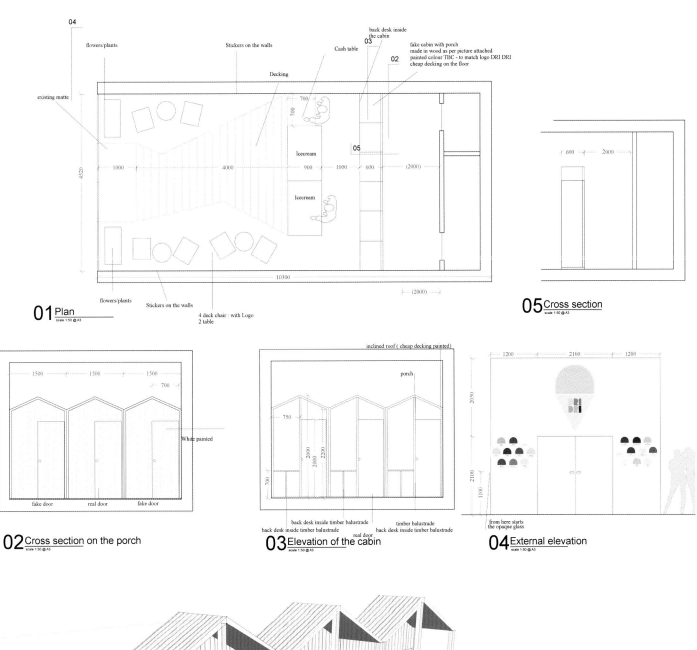

04

flowers/plants

Stickers on the walls

Cash table

Decking

back desk inside
the cabin

03

02

fake cabin with porch
made in wood as per picture attached
painted colour TBC - to match logo DRI DRI
cheap decking on the floor

existing matte

700

700

Icecream

05

900

1000

600

(2000)

4520

1000

4000

Icecream

10300

(2000)

flowers/plants

Stickers on the walls

4 deck chair : with Logo
2 table

01 Plan
scale 1:50 @ A3

05 Cross section
scale 1:50 @ A3

600

2000

02 Cross section on the porch
scale 1:50 @ A3

1500

1500

1500

700

White painted

fake door

real door

fake door

03 Elevation of the cabin
scale 1:50 @ A3

inclined roof (cheap decking painted)

porch

750

2600
2000
2200

700

back desk inside timber balustrade
back desk inside timber balustrade

timber balustrade
back desk inside timber balustrade

real door

04 External elevation
scale 1:50 @ A3

1200

2100

1200

2050

2100

1100

from here starts
the opaque glass

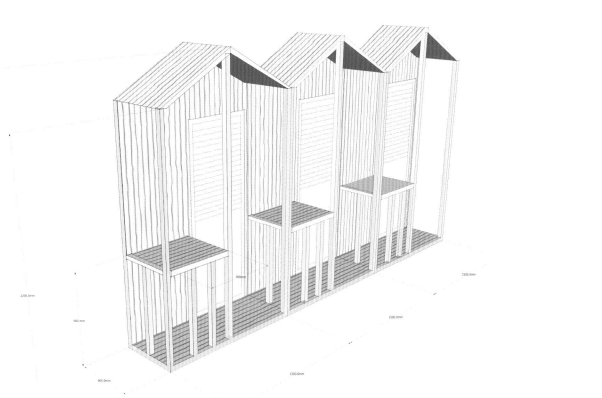

2200.0mm

900 mm

600.0mm

700mm

1500.0mm

1500.0mm

1500.0mm

1500.0mm

Phill Nuca Studio

Location: Ilfov, Romania **Photography:** Cosmin Dragomir

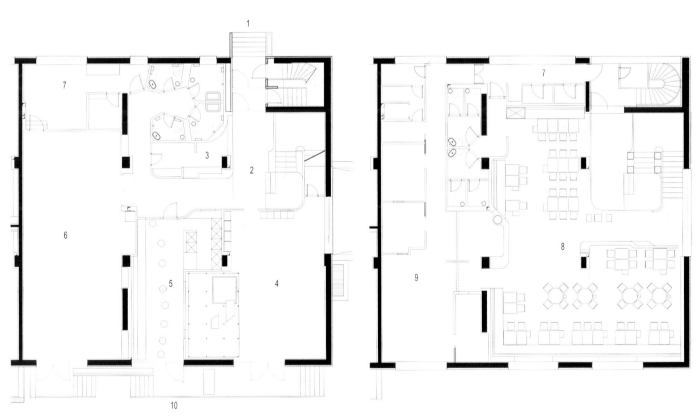

Ground Floor   First Floor

Phill is a meeting place designed for the entire family. It has a playground, a multipurpose room and a small café at the ground floor and a gourmet restaurant at the first level.

The playground and the multipurpose room are enclosed areas with independent light and acoustic scenarios and they accommodate activities from theater and puppet shows to martial arts and ballet lessons. Upstairs, the dining area is an open space directly linked with the lobby. In between them the small café communicates visually with the playground through a couple of round openings. The functions of the program have their own agenda but at the same time they work closely together therefore the connection of the individual spaces was very important. In order to link these different rooms, the walls were perforated by transparent openings and a special attention was paid to the stairs design which climb their way to the first floor around a four meter tall elephant.

The space's layout was mostly determined by: dividing two groups of activities specific to both kids and adults, binding the two, distributing the space on the two levels and the lavish backyard.

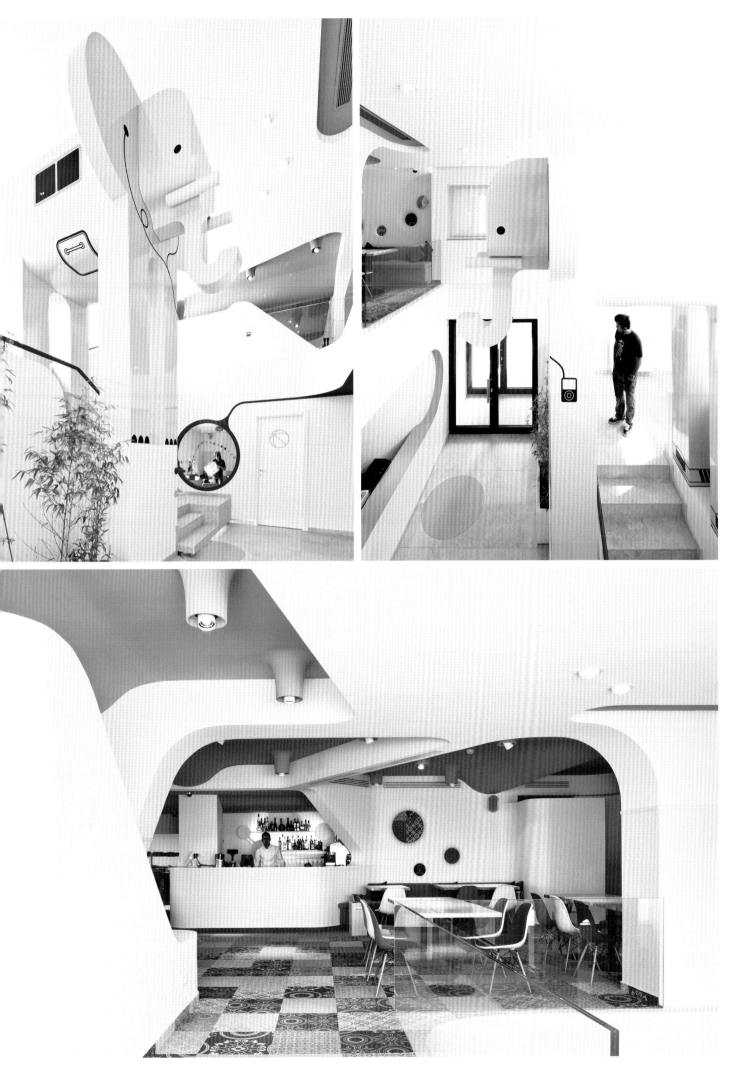

GREEN BISTRO Jörn Fröhlich, Siddik Erdogan

Location: Osnabrück, Germany **Floor Area:** 100 sqm **Completion Year:** 2011 **Photography:** Siddik Erdogan

green bistro

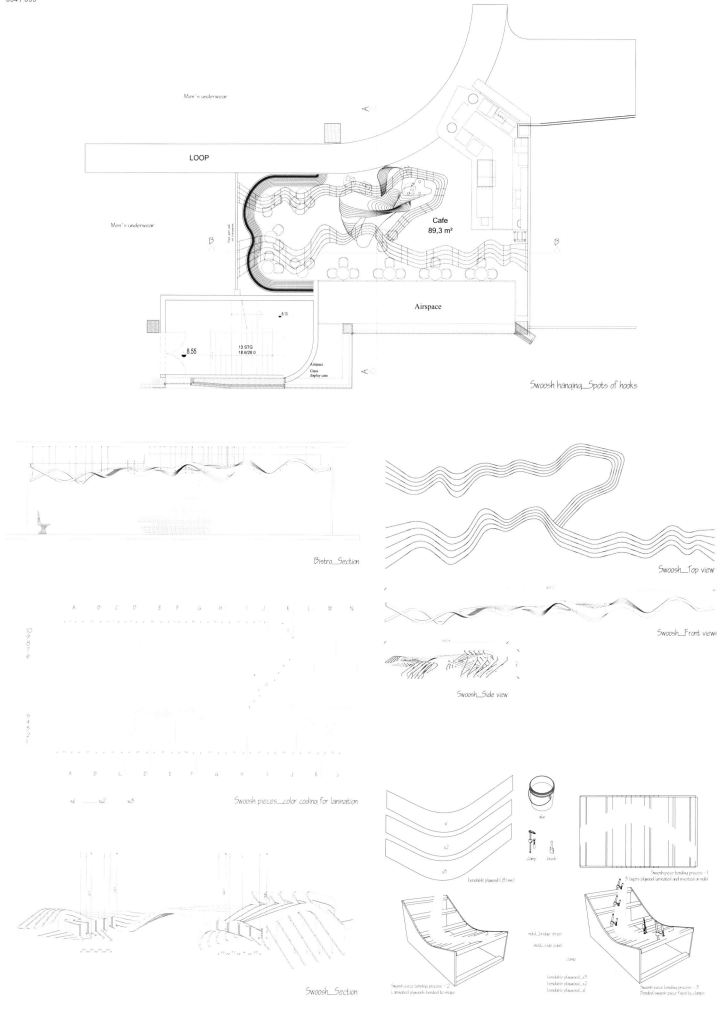

Men's underwear

LOOP

Men's underwear

Cafe
89,3 m²

Airspace

6.13

8.55

13 STG
18.6/26.0

Airspace
Glass
display case

Swoosh hanging_Spots of hooks

Bistro_Section

Swoosh_Top view

Swoosh_Front view

Swoosh_Side view

Swoosh pieces_color coding for lamination

Swoosh_Section

bendable plywood (8 mm)

Swoosh piece bending process - 1
3 layers plywood laminated and inserted on mold

Swoosh piece bending process - 2
Laminated plywoods bended to shape

Swoosh piece bending process - 3
Bended swoosh piece fixed by clamps

The GREEN BISTRO interior design at LENGERMANN & TRIESCHMANN DEPT. STORE, Osnabrück, Germany is the result of international design cooperation between Jörn Fröhlich (theatre and retail design, Berlin - Germany) and Siddik Erdogan (interior designer, Izmir - Turkey).

The basic concept evolves around the lifestyle of health and sustainability promoting healthy green food items to the customers. The choice of material reflects that idea. As design inspirations the team chose organic shapes derived from nature itself avoiding any kind of rectangular forms or sharp edges. The materials consist of naturally enhanced plywood combined with white lacquered surfaces. All functional parts such as food displays, tray shelves, benches and tables have been merged into overall organically shaped objects that have been designed, planned and manufactured individually.

In order to add a sophisticated touch to the organic design idea, white pantone chairs and white tulip tables have been installed.

To complete the team's conceptual vision a ceiling centerpiece covering all 100m² of the bistro area has been created. As a complex wavy structured object it has been uniquely developed and installed without opening up the existing suspended ceiling. The manufacturing process of that object was a delicate and challenging procedure and the result is worth seeing when visiting Osnabrück in Germany.

Slade Architecture designed the Barbie Café and B-Bar on the sixth floor of the Barbie Flagship store in Shanghai, China as an immersive dining experience intended to expand on the overall Barbie Flagship Store experience.

To accommodate the different ages and atmospheres, Slade chose a simple and striking palette: black lacquer, white accents, pink upholstery and curtains. Slade designed the custom herringbone tile pattern on the floors and walls to recall the herringbone swimsuit that Barbie first wore when she debuted at the New York Toy Fair in 1959.

Furniture was also designed by Slade Architecture which includes acrylic chairs printed with whimsical silhouette of iconic chairs: one Chinese antique, one European antique, one international modern design. These silhouette prints create a literal blend of the café's references. Table bases are flat cutout silhouettes of classic turned wood profiles.

By day the Barbie Café provides a perfect place for tasty lunch or enchanting dinner. The sexy B Bar, a sculptural black bar under a hanging mobile of Barbie icon cut-outs rocks until 2am, serving an alluring menu of creative cocktails –BarbieTinis and Malibu Barbies – to real-life glamour girls and their attendant Kens.

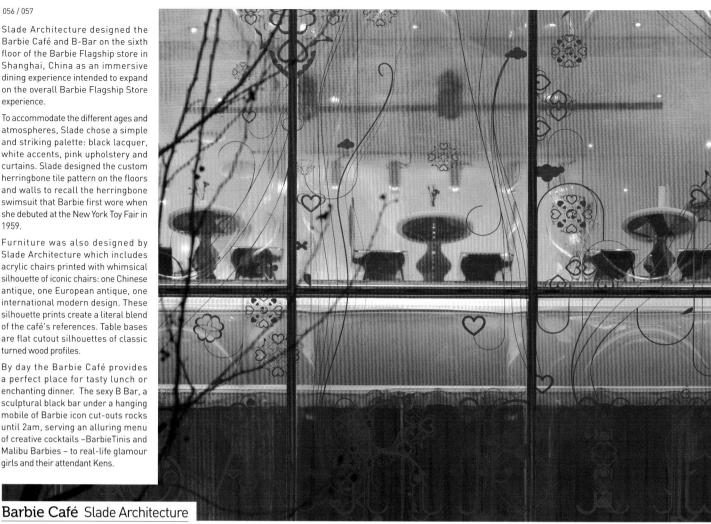

Barbie Café Slade Architecture

Location: Shanghai, China **Floor Area:** 420 sqm (90 sqm café and 330 sqm restaurant) **Completion Year:** 2009 **Photography:** Iwan Baan

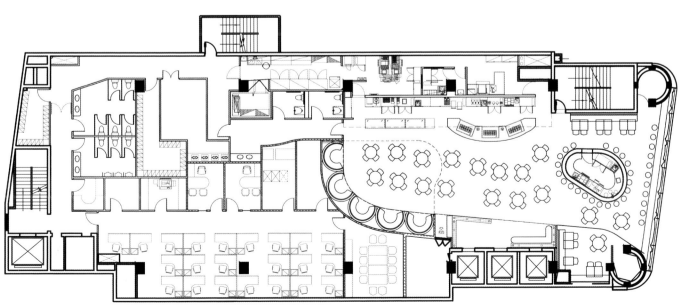

PLAN

'Living Lab': PizzaExpress, Richmond Ab Rogers Design

Location: Richmond, UK **Floor Area:** 365 sqm **Completion Year:** 2010 **Photography:** John Short

The designers took PizzaExpress back to its original essence, celebrating the joy of eating good food and the theatre of traditional pizza making, while bringing light back into the restaurant, giving it an injection of color and excitement. They put the kitchen and all its vibrant activity under the spotlight; centre stage in a space that excites the senses. Parabolic lighting domes - created in collaboration with leading acoustician Sergio Luzzi - help create localize sound pockets around each table. Built-in speakers allow customers to play music from their own iPods; diners can dim their own lights or press a "light-up" button to ask for the bill. A long, undulating counter connects the dining area with the kitchen, where mouth-watering ingredients sit in tidy rows, pizzaiolos toss dough high into the air, and delicious aromas waft from a fiery oven. To bring in a family clientele throughout the day, they interspersed kids' activity areas throughout the restaurant, including interactive stealth learning games (pizza-themed, of course) and a large communal drawing table. Inspired by the open stalls of Naples, they punched a kiosk through to the street, allowing passersby to grab food and drink on the move. The first restaurant was treated as a living lab where designers could test new concepts, monitor public response and explore the outer limits of what a PizzaExpress can be.

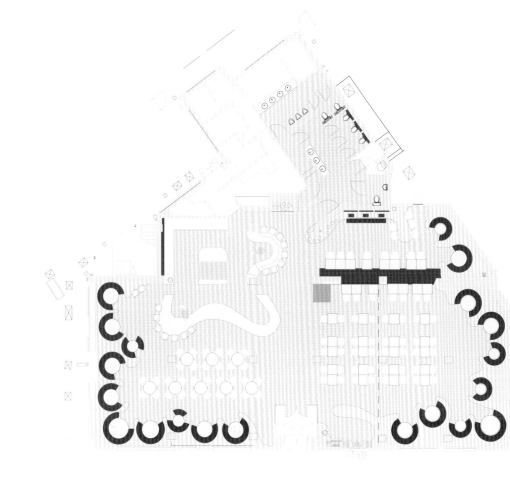

Fastvínic Alfons Tost Interiorisme

Location: Barcelona, Spain **Floor Area:** 142.3 sqm **Completion Year:** 2011 **Photography:** Eugeni Pons

Fastvinic was born as an environmental and sustainable project, as well as a functional space where the customers could flow around the space enjoying the self-service concept.

The space has two levels, the ground floor with kitchen and dinning-room and the underground with bathrooms and service office.

On the ground floor there is a perimetral element, a "mecano shelves" resoling the requirements of each space; seats in the dinning-room, bar in the corridor, support the wine and recycling machines and the higher part of the shelves are supporting the plants referring the compromise with the nature and helping the regeneration of the oxygen.

All the elements are designed to be recycled and dismantable. The kitchen, located on the entrance is designed as a domestic space because of the colors and the materials, and has the intention to work as window-shopping where the customers could enjoy watching the domestic process of the kitchen before choosing the menu.

On the underground, there are two big elements covered with pine wood forming the service areas.

Sustainability is found in all levels; on the materials, eco, woods FSC (from under control forest), adhesive free of volatile carcinogenic... the designers recover all the grey water of the energetic waste. All the lighting of the space is with electrical appliance Leeds. Even the final product that they provide to the customers – the packaging is also 100% compostable.

CONTESTO ALIMENTARE POINT.

Location: Torino, Italy **Floor Area:** 60 sqm **Completion Year:** 2012 **Photography:** Enrico Muraro

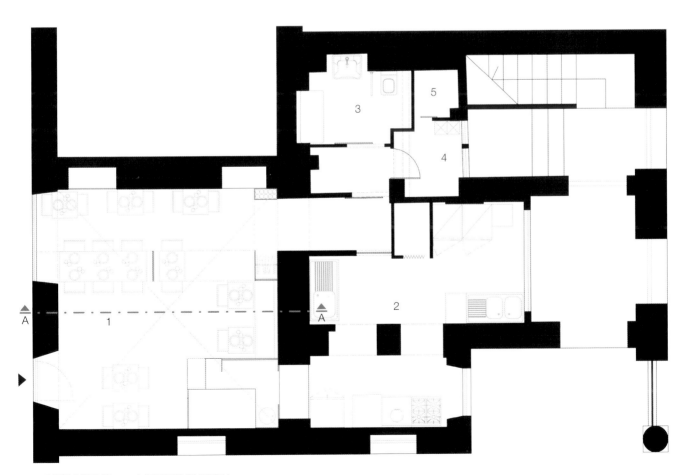

1. RESTAURANT
2. KITCHEN
3. TOILET
4. DRESSING ROOM
5. STORAGE ROOM

0m   0.5m   1m   2m

The project wants to convey the traditional old fashioned restaurant atmosphere into a contemporary design space, where the core is the big cupboard opposite to the entrance. Made of white lacquered and natural matte medium density wood, this object is intended to be both a functional element to organize the space (wardrobe, shelves, seating, counter are inside it) and the only decorative piece in the room. Its design focuses on the idea of open and closed drawers: each part of the furniture is thus conceived according to this idea, and also the big crossing suspended volume that ends on the outside. The oversize sofa refines the style of this cosy and warm restaurant, welcoming the guests.

Together with the architectural project, POINT. developed also the corporate identity. It points out the evolution of the classic Italian "trattoria". In a minimalist style the brand recalls the gates of the old taverns while the lettering resumes in a modern style typical signs of the last century. Brown is the main color of this graphic project, having been used also for the architectural design details (wood, sofas, walls).

Caffè di Mezzo JM Architecture

Location: Castelfranco Veneto, Italy **Floor Area:** 200 sqm **Completion Year:** 2009 **Photography:** Jacopo Mascheroni

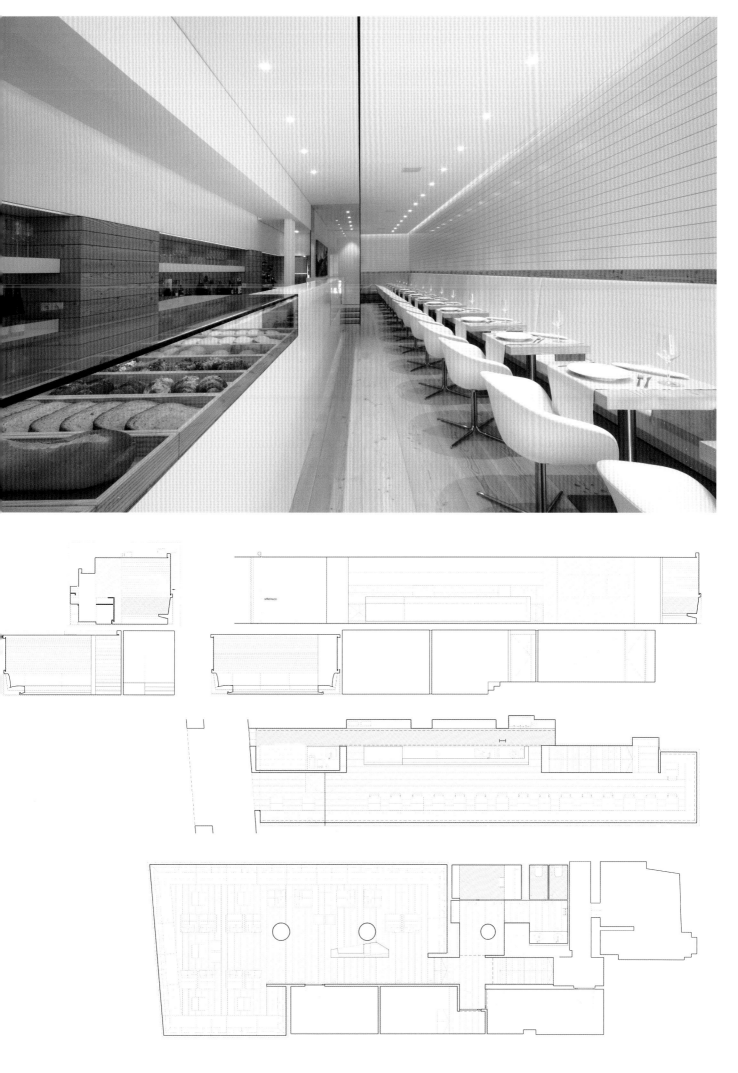

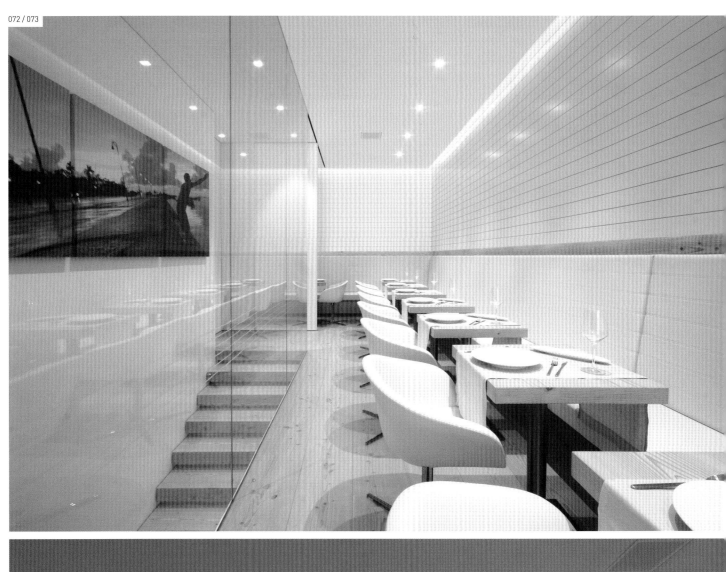

The line guide for the remodelling of the Caffè di Mezzo, located in Castelfranco Veneto near Treviso, is the idea of creating an essential space, defined by linear design, simple geometries and light effects, with the intent of conferring it a certain elegance and balance. The space, located on the ground floor of a twentieth-century building, overlooks the arcades surrounding a beautiful medieval castle, which contains the historic centre of Giorgione's hometown. The main feature of this bar is its twenty meter long rectangular shape. The project therefore emphasizes the longitudinal original shape creating an important sense of perspective. Another important feature of the space is the skylight, which opens into an inner courtyard of the building. This element plays a significant role in the architectural composition, giving great character to the bar service area below it. The new space is organized in two functional areas: the first, for service, is defined by a long linear counter, 1.2 meters high, clad in white Corian and with a bottom light cove which grants it a sense of lightness to the space. The second area is the one reserved to the customers, and it's characterized by a bench upholstered in white leather which runs longitudinally and turns around the walls at the end to emphasize the continuity and wrap the space as much as possible. Aligned with the main counter is a white Corian full height block, which also serves as a perimeter wall corresponding to the exterior private setback space for the bar customers, by setting back the transparent glass enclosure.

Plachuttas Gasthaus zur Oper Atelier Heiss Architekten

Location: Vienna, Austria **Floor Area:** 630 sqm **Completion Year:** 2011 **Photography:** Philipp Kreidl

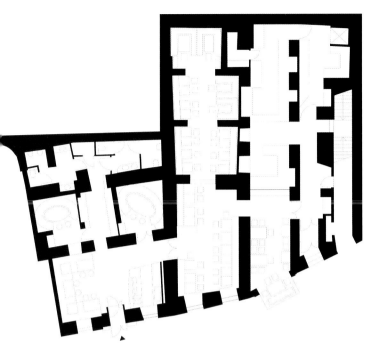

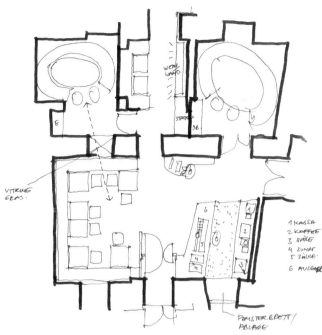

F-01-Grundriss-EG
F-02 Grundriss EG-ohne Gastgarten

Skizze-Ovale

The extensive reconstruction of the historic building, which is in part protected as a historic monument, and the joining of two buildings was mastered by Atelier Heiss Architekten with great sensitivity.

The traditional Gasthaus terms are reinterpreted in a new manner and now evoke a modern flair, featuring glazed, sculpted tiles, elaborately restored wainscoting as well as subdued color shades.

Specially designed solid wood tables embody the claim to highest quality, emphasizing the proximity to the Ballet of the Vienna State Opera by its "dancing table legs".

The variety of dining areas is brought together to a harmonious whole by the continuous design and a clear axis through the rooms. The reception and bar area leads to two elliptical private rooms, which provide cozy tables for the regulars. The main dining room features vaults dating back to medieval times, and yet has a distinctly urban atmosphere with a reinforced foundation. The Kitchen Room completes the restaurant, allowing a view of the busy happenings in the kitchen and simultaneous enjoyment of the square outside.

A further highlight is the outdoor seating area with an impressive awning, giving the public area a new design and upgrading by premium-quality granite and new lighting, revitalizing this neighborhood of downtown Vienna.

Alara Restaurant Marcos Samaniego / Mas Arquitectura

Location: La Coruna, Spain **Floor Area:** 596 sqm **Completion Year:** 2011 **Photography:** Ana Samaniego

Alara, a restaurant located in Finisterre, Spain, mixes design and tradition in a unique building.

Finisterre has always been a magical place. Today this fishing village retains its exotic charm. A square, which crowns a small harbor, welcomes weary travelers. This is where Alara Finisterre emerges.

Redesigning an old house, Marcos Samaniego, architect of Mas Arquitectura, has developed a spectacular complex with cafe, restaurant and tavern.

Each room has been carefully designed in order to create different atmospheres. Finisterre´s fishing essence is presented in front of the local through big photos whilst turned lining offers a design contrast. In addition, lighting has been individualized to emphasize Alara Finisterre's characteristics. A terrace has been designed with a bench in order to take advantage of Atlantic sea views.

Alara Finisterre has already become a gastronomic and architectural referent, a place that only a few are able to enjoy.

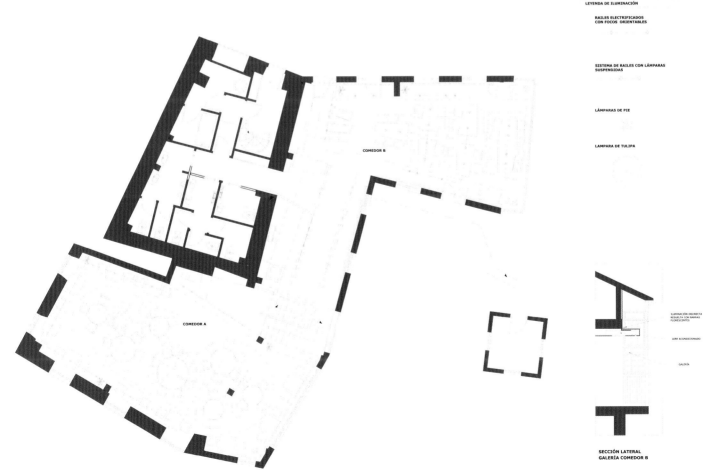

LEYENDA DE ILUMINACIÓN

RAILES ELECTRIFICADOS CON FOCOS ORIENTABLES

SISTEMA DE RAILES CON LÁMPARAS SUSPENDIDAS

LÁMPARAS DE PIE

LAMPARA DE TULIPA

COMEDOR B

ILUMINACIÓN INDIRECTA RESUELTA CON BARRAS FLORESCENTES

AIRE ACONDICIONADO

GALERÍA

COMEDOR A

SECCIÓN LATERAL GALERÍA COMEDOR B

nivel 1 iluminacion

smith&hsu Teahouse in Taipei Carsten Jörgensen

Location: Taiwan China **Floor Area:** 172 sqm **Completion Year:** 2011 **Photography:** Alain Kuan

smith&hsu's teahouse on Nan Jing Road in Taipei is the 5th and latest addition to the brand. Envisioned by Swiss / Danish designer Carsten Jörgensen, the new teahouse has two floors seating 48 guests in the upper dining area and 10 guests in the spacious lower tea shop. It carries minimalistic tea tools exclusively created for smith&hsu and its outstanding teas.

The wood and concrete interior feels authentic. The materials chosen for the store reflect the subtlety of a great tea and trigger the guests' aesthetic sensibility. In keeping with modernistic principles of visual clarity and simplicity, Carsten Jörgensen has created a wonderful framework for experiencing quality teas. The teahouse's ascetic yet warm charm has a calming effect even after one of those long and stressful days.

As an extension of the design for the previous smith&hsu teahouses, the key elements of the new store are "soil" and "wood". The store's concrete surfaces display a subtle spectrum of grayish, bluish, yellowish and brownish colors. Concrete walls and floors add an earthy feel, whereas the wood gives the store a sense of organic warmth. All the materials smith&hsu has used for the teahouse feel refreshingly raw and uncluttered.

Bookshelves made of piles of wooden cubes run around the walls of the entire second floor, creating an open library for smith&hsu's guests. The tea and the books, the concrete and the wood somehow all make sense together in this great looking new teahouse. smith&hsu has managed to combine asceticism with homeliness and the result is best described as something akin to wisdom.

Ator Restaurant Expose ARCHITECTURE and DESIGN

Location: Tehran, Iran **Floor Area:** 50 sqm **Completion Year:** 2011 **Photography:** Saeed Azadi

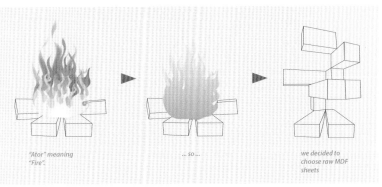

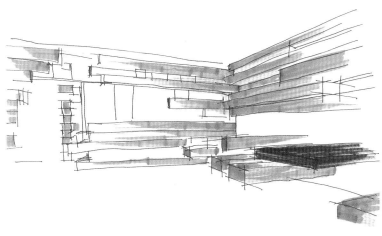

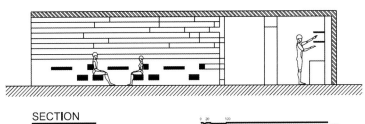

SECTION

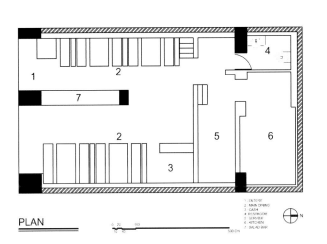

PLAN

1. ENTERY
2. MAIN DINING
3. CASH
4. RESTROOM
5. SERVICE
6. KITCHEN
7. SALAD BAR

Ator is a 50-square-meter restaurant which was established in 2010 in Tehran, Iran. From the start of the design process it struggled with many needs and requests of the employers. For example, the owner requested that, cleaning under tables should be simple and easy. Or because of the bad location of the restaurant and being far from the main street, people couldn't maintain a good view of the street from the inside of the restaurant, so the architects decided to design the tables and chairs in the way that they didn't have any legs, so the cleaning would be easy...

The Tastings Room Studio SKLIM

Location: Marina Square, Singapore **Floor Area:** 137 sqm **Completion Year:** 2011 **Photography:** Jeremy San, Studio SKLIM

The Tastings Room is a new addition to the heart of Singapore's Central Business District, Marina Square with the fine combination of French/Italian bistro cuisine and wine cellar under one roof. The restaurant's vision was to refresh the perception of wine and food culture in Singapore by providing them at affordable prices. The overall spatial experience sandwiches the crafted black volumes between two layers of industrial aesthetics: exposed ceiling and concrete screed floor, to juxtapose/merge opposing aesthetics of being sophisticated yet affordable.

The programmatic composition was divided into three areas namely Wine, Bistro and shared spaces of Wine/Bistro. A U-shaped band of these programs was deployed as it provided the most flexible layout with regards to shared functions, main circulation and points of entry/exit. The Central Bar sits firmly in the middle to negotiate the needs of Wine and Bistro, as well as providing the point of sales for this establishment.

Drawing inspiration from the outer aesthetics of the dark wine bottle and antique weaved wine basket holders, the outer skin of these volumes adopt a series of black diagonal tiles while the interiors are inspired by the "hidden" flavors of wine, taking on singular hues for rooms such as the ruby wine cellar and amber kitchen.

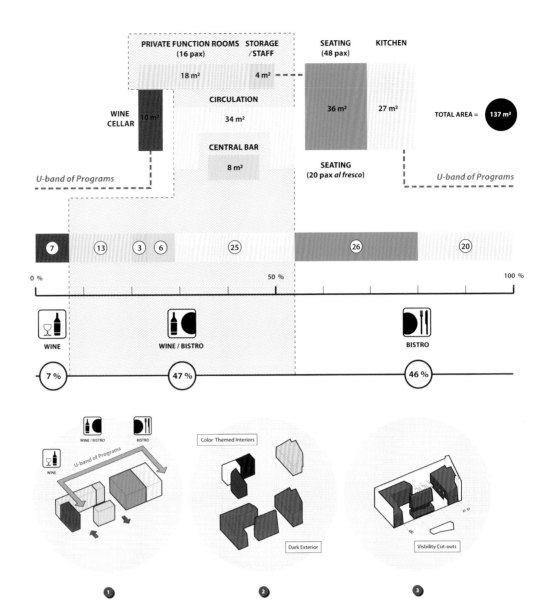

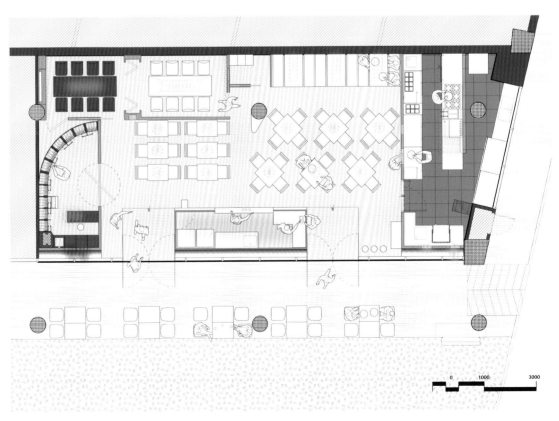

Kenting Tea House Beige Design Ltd.

Location: Hong Kong, China **Floor Area:** 4,000 sq ft **Completion Year:** 2010 **Photography:** Ulso Tsang

Beige Design Ltd. brings in modern retro-chic to a Taiwan Cafe on a scooter, scooting around in exotic mood, getting caught by the sense of retrospective Taiwan in a modern setting, and indulging in the imagery of white and blue.

Led by the seashore odor of the natural rustic ship-wood on the ceiling, the raw but stylish details start telling their stories in a casual way.

The open food counter which is wrapped by blackboard panels designed for food menu and free hand-writing. Everybody sit under the bubble-like pendant lights, which resonate with the rendered nostalgic Taiwan elements on the deck.

The circular booth seating, short and long tables and party seating caters for all customers from heart-chat to group party.

There lies a key color of sky blue outlining the contour of exoticism and nostalgia beside the sea.

Highlighted by the scooter at the entrance and the lighthouse image at the far end, the interior of the cafe demonstrates successful memory relocation and the localization of cultural elements with design.

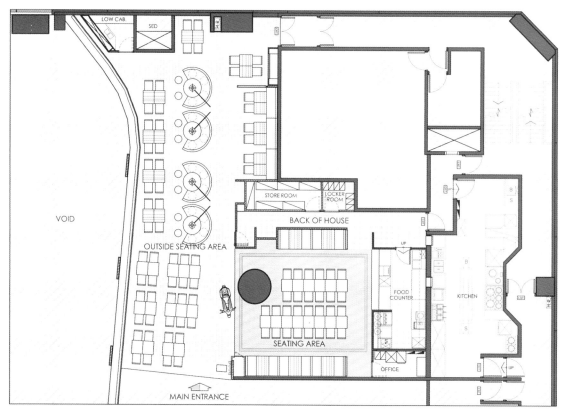

Floor plan labels:

LOW CAB.

SED

VOID

OUTSIDE SEATING AREA

STORE ROOM

LOCKER ROOM

BACK OF HOUSE

SEATING AREA

FOOD COUNTER

KITCHEN

OFFICE

UP

MAIN ENTRANCE

FLOOR PLAN

What Happens When - Temporary Restaurant Movement 2 Elle Kunnos de Voss, The Metrics

Location: New York, USA **Floor Area:** 1,200 sq ft **Completion Year:** 2011 **Photography:** Felix de Voss

What Happens When is a temporary restaurant installation that transforms every 30 days to explore what a dining experience can be and how we can play with the traditional expectations of dining out. Chef John Fraser creates a new menu each month, Elle Kunnos de Voss designs a new interior and a new composer is invited to create a unique sound scope for each month.

With the forest/ where the wild things is the theme of the interior design concept for Movement 2, which is taking on a play with scale. The space is defined by an installation of over-sized pine needles that create a movement across the ceiling. Stretching to the floor in some areas the pine needles act as room dividers.

Throughout the space little moments unveil the fantastical forest theme such as two moss-laden swings with miniature landscapes of plants and birds, bird houses nestled in the pine needles and various animal tracks on the floor, walls and selected tables.

The over table pendants are made from a sheet of stationary held together with a single staple. The stationary, screen printed bird motif on vintage typing paper, is designed by Adrienne Wong. The counter area light fixtures are made with live moss and small bulbs.

What Happens When - Temporary Restaurant SILK ROAD Elle Kunnos de Voss, The Metrics

Location: New York, USA **Floor Area:** 1,200 sq ft **Completion Year:** 2011 **Photography:** Felix de Voss

Initiated by Chef John Fraser, What Happens When is a temporary restaurant installation that transforms every 30 days to explore what a dining experience can be and how we can play with the traditional expectations of dining out.

For this 5th transformation the interior takes its inspiration from Silk Road.

The Metrics collected patterns from regions spanning from Turkey to China to create a maze of screens made from 30x30cm large cardboard panels. The panels have laser cut patterns collected from various regions of the Silk Road: Turkey, Babylon, Syria, Uzbekistan, Turkmenistan, Afghanistan and two different regions of China.

The panels are hanging from the ceiling hooks in formations from the entry going east, starting with patterns from Turkey stretching all the way through the space ending in the two different China patterns. Throughout the panels act as room dividers and are hung around light fixtures creating a play of light and shadow. The panels are spray painted in colors ranging from sand and light blues, through turquoise to the deep red of China.

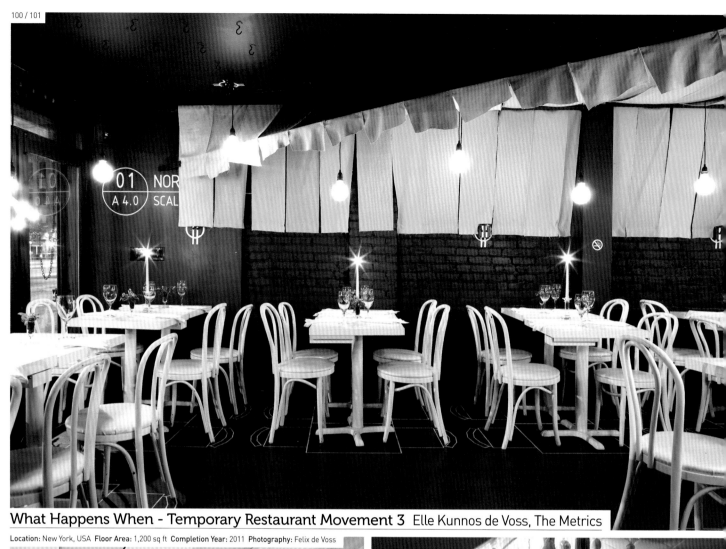

What Happens When - Temporary Restaurant Movement 3 Elle Kunnos de Voss, The Metrics

Location: New York, USA **Floor Area:** 1,200 sq ft **Completion Year:** 2011 **Photography:** Felix de Voss

Initiated by Chef John Fraser, What Happens When is a temporary restaurant installation that transforms every 30 days to explore what a dining experience can be and how we can play with the traditional expectations of dining out.

The 3rd transformation takes on a spring garden party theme inspired by Renoir's "The Luncheon of the Boating Party".

The interiors draw a few significant elements and from the Renoir painting to recreate an intimate, communal experience reminiscent of 19th century time and place. A 25' awning like architectural stroke across the room frames the dining settings in warm spring like tones to recreate the communal intimate feeling of the painting.

The ceiling is lit with a "garden party" string light inspired configuration of bulbs. To create a play between interior and exterior, elements such as branch-like light fixtures and iconic Still life wall sconces nod both to nature and the genre of painting. Throughout the space, guests will likewise discover details that reference the time period, such as 1900s inspired graphics across the tables and period pieces.

The bathrooms are divided between male and female interpretations of the time period, drawing inspiration from a boudoir and harbor graphics respectively.

Mikkeller bar Femmes Regionales

Location: Copenhagen, Denmark **Floor Area:** 100 sqm **Completion Year:** 2010 **Photography:** Lars Engelgaar

The Danish design agency Femmes Regionales, who's the creative mind behind the interior, had the ambition of combining the classic interior of old Danish pubs with something more modern and elegant: "Just like Mikkeller has combined the old profession of brewing with more innovative and experimenting methods," Caroline Hansen, one of the founders of Femmes Regionales, explains. With her companion Mie Nielsen, she went pub-crawling in the centre of Copenhagen to collect some inspiration. "We found the contrast between the classical pub interior and something more modern really interesting," the designer says. The result is a relaxed yet sophisticated whole with wooden tables and benches, a shiny wall of black tiles and details of golden lamps, knobs, coat hooks and flowers in dusty colors.

All in all the bar is not quite as manly as most beer places, and Femmes Regionales wanted to add a twist of solemness to the place as well, which they - among other things - did by designing a row of small chests of drawers with mirrors and golden knobs that they hung on the wall, Caroline Hansens explains: "If there is something a bit solemn to a place, people won't bang their fists in the tables and empty their glasses in one, but behave in a different manner. We like to demand something from our audience – beauty generates beauty."

Coutume Café CUT Architectures

Location: Paris, France **Floor Area:** 90 sqm **Completion Year:** 2011 **Photography:** David Foessel, Luc Boegly

CUT Architectures designed the first Coutume Café in the centre of Paris combining a roastery and a café offering the best coffees in Paris and a neat selection of fresh and organic food and delicacies.

In the spirit of specialty coffee, the experts at Coutume give the opportunity to rediscover the coffee culture with high-end tools and machines.

The blend of tradition, alchemy and technique inspired CUT Architectures' design.

Tearing down the walls and ceilings brought back a typical Parisian interior with high ceilings, moldings, columns and an old shop door. New oak flooring adds up to the Parisian atmosphere.

CUT Architectures set in this decor a laboratory of coffee using square white tiles, grid lighting, stainless steel, industrial plastic curtains, and laboratory glassware.

The plain oak tables were designed for Coutume as the fusion of this Parisian interior and laboratory.

Capanna k-studio

Location: Athens, Greece **Floor Area:** 90 sqm **Completion Year:** 2011 **Photography:** Yiorgos Kordakis

The experience of eating outside was the starting point for the design of Capanna. The aim was to render the space with the atmosphere of an Italian courtyard. A pallet made up of materials familiarly found in these spaces such as cement tiles, stucco plaster, travertine stone, blackened steel railings, and characteristic narrow wooden shutters, were used to clad the different spaces in the restaurant. The wood burning oven and the pizza bar are enclosed within a travertine stone box that sits in the far corner of the place framing the Pizzaiolo. On top of it balances a rectangular volume, clad with reclaimed wooden shutters, enclosing the kitchen, storage and WC facilities. The two shapes connect with a suspended steel staircase that penetrates them. The floor is laid with grey cement tiles but in the double-height area of the restaurant geometrically patterned cement tiles create a carpet-like strip that continues onto the adjacent wall, emphasizing the height of the room. The various vintage chairs add softness and a laid-back feeling to the restaurant and the grey stucco plastered walls and ceiling help to enclose all of this in a textured, minimal envelope.

The combination of purposefully designed elements, reclaimed materials and vintage furniture, presents an architecture that sits comfortably between the bespoke and the sourced, creating an exciting and sociable atmosphere.

BARREL Kamitov Project

Location: Almaty, Kazakhstan **Floor Area:** 600 sqm **Completion Year:** 2011

BARREL Bar is located at the central part of the city, at the ground floor of Hotel OTRAR ALMATY. It's a full reconstruction with a capacity of 170 people. The kitchen and bar area is 600 square meters. It is open from 11:30am till 2am. The concept of the project is "freedom" and "democracy" and simplicity is a principle.

According to the idea of concept, Kamitov Project used simple and useful materials in the furniture, lightings and wall decoration. The bar has a stage for live band and dance area. Each part has their own identity.

Barrio 47 bluarch architecture + interiors +lighting

Location: New York, USA Floor Area: 1,200 sq ft Completion Year: 2012 Photography: ADO

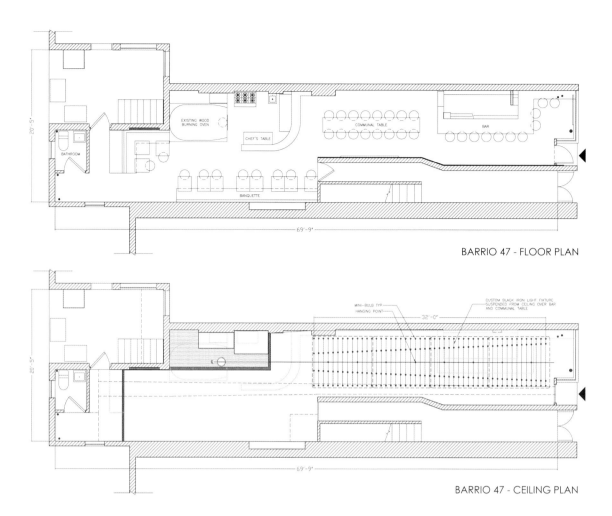

BARRIO 47 - FLOOR PLAN

BARRIO 47 - CEILING PLAN

Barrio 47, a new tapas restaurant, has now joined the West Village's hip restaurant circuit. Designed by bluarch architecture + interiors + lighting, the restaurant's hand-painted murals were chosen to remain in the new design, while the opposite south-facing wall within the bar areas has now been clad in plaster of varying tones of warm neutrals and then adorned with a laser cut feature and affixed with rivets. Subway tiles in black and deep green have been applied to all other vertical surfaces.

A custom made iron chandelier lit by 1/2" incandescent light bulbs span the length of the bar area, establishing two separate areas for the bar and for dining. The back dining area is lit by linear pendant lighting. The place is energized by the controlled doses of red on the bar stools and brick oven, and further enlivened by the white Carrara marble bar and table tops.

pulpeira Marcos Samaniego / Mas Arquitectura

Location: Madrid, Spain Floor Area: 106 sqm Completion Year: 2008/2011 Photography: Ana Samaniego

A unique place to share experiences and enjoy tasty dinner, this is "pulpeira", a traditional Galician restaurant where octopus is the main product. The project, developed by Marcos Samaniego from Mas Arquitectura, adapts this traditional store to an urban space in Madrid.

The local, called it "Pulpeira Vilalúa", which follows a main idea – a place to share your time with family and friends. For this reason, the local has designed continuous benches – an invitation to share experiences - and perimetral layout. The furniture, designed by Mas Arquitectura team, bets for renewable materials, such as old wood.

The entrance to "Vilalúa" universe supposes a trip to the unknown world: the pleasure of good cooking. A tunnel, which allows people to entry in the local, has been equipped with shelves and wastebaskets to turn this space into a comfortable place for smokers.

Inside, the local hides a lot of secrets. A special main door or wine barrels used as tables are interesting details that should be discovered.

Mas Arquitectura, a Spanish young study, has developed this project from design to execution. Only this way of working guarantees a perfect harmony: furniture, lighting and layout are part of a set of "Pulpeira Vilalúa".

Jaffa – Tel Aviv Restaurant Baranowitz Kronenberg Architects

Location: Tel Aviv, Israel **Floor Area:** 350 sqm **Completion Year:** 2011 **Photography:** Amit Geron

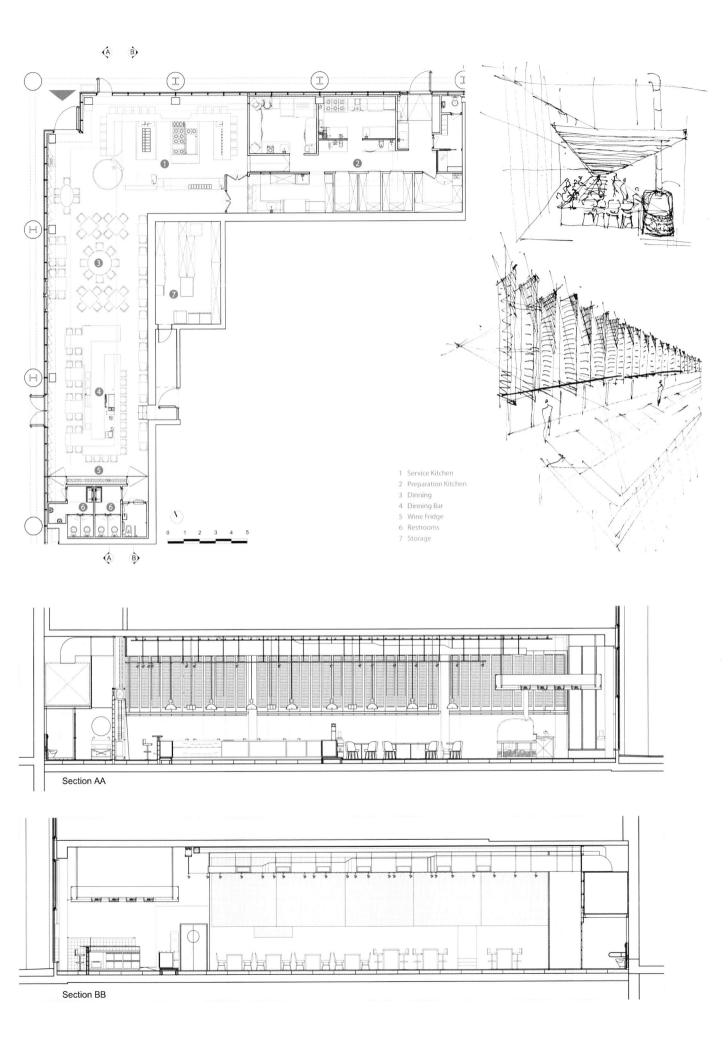

1 Service Kitchen
2 Preparation Kitchen
3 Dinning
4 Dinning Bar
5 Wine Fridge
6 Restrooms
7 Storage

0 1 2 3 4 5

Section AA

Section BB

Haim Cohen, the chef who reinvented the Israeli cuisine, appointed BK Architects for the design of his new restaurant. In Israel many culinary traditions live together, Cohen brings them to an utterly fresh level of cuisine.

BK Architects started off at the same point as Haim with an aim to represent the spirit of his kitchen. Using simplicity and honesty as primer building materials they make use of raw and ordinary finishes, however, they are only their starting point. The restaurant envelop is done with the very basic materials: water, cement, aggregates and steel. Exactly as Haim's cuisine: water, flour and olive oil.

The exposed concrete walls of the envelop were polished to reveal the true nature of the stone aggregates, while the concrete floor and ceiling were left untouched. Like the culinary ingredients which come from different lands, many design elements are mixed together.

They evoke not only the essence of Cohen's kitchen but also the flair of the old Jaffa, a city where multi-national traditions live side by side. The mix of different elements provides a sophisticated representation of a cultural melting pot.

The wide space is divided in three areas: the poured terrazzo alcohol bar, the dining hall and the open kitchen which is the embodiment of "hospitality". Guests are invited to sit around the burning fire and watch the "show", while the kitchen's stainless steel tops become a huge dining bar.

Dishoom Afroditi Krassa

Location: London, UK **Floor Area:** 5,000 sq ft **Completion Year:** 2010 **Photography:** Sim Canetty-Clarke

Designed by Afroditi Krassa, the designer behind Itsu, in conjunction with Dishoom's owner Shamil Thakrar, the 5,000 square feet venue is a contemporary and unexpected interpretation of a traditional Irani cafe. Drawing on Bombay's rich past, street stalls and down-to-earth eateries, the interior combines elegant, sophisticated and simple lines with the city's art deco past. Custom-made checkerboard tiles, oak paneling, white Carrara marble – topped tables and mismatched chairs create a relaxed, democratic café-style space. Antique mirrors, slowly turning ceiling fans, a monochromatic color palette, a lighting scheme that includes bespoke glass orbs by Rothchild & Bickers and a feature wall by Deborah Bowness all contribute to a modern, light and airy space that evokes vintage Bombay but is most definitely present day London, with retro portraiture and 60s pop art drawing a parallel with London's own past. Contrasting with the traditional curry house, Afroditi's design also represents an evolution in British diners' perceptions of the environment to eat food from the subcontinent in, with flock wallpaper and sitar music but a distant memory. Even the name "Dishoom", an old Bollywood expression rather like Pow! or Bam! encapsulates the energy of the concept and design.

Afroditi Proposed General Arrangement Plan
(Ground Floor)

Afroditi Proposed General Arrangement Plan
(Basement)

Pompei's Restaurant and Gelato Bar Luigi Rosselli Architects

Location: Sydney, Australia **Floor Area:** 150 sqm **Completion Year:** 2011 **Photography:** Yann Audic

Luigi Rosselli Architects' latest venture into the culinary landscape sees the Venetian backdrop of George Pompei's childhood transplanted into the eclectic surroundings of Bondi Beach, Australia. Inspired by John Ruskin's exploratory text The Stones of Venice, the design channels the Byzantine use of tiles, mosaic and mirror that is characteristic of the Gothic architecture of Venice. The cool fresh colors of the tiles in the main dining room cast eyes outwards to the marine landscape of Bondi Beach beyond. In contrast, a second more private dining room at the back looks inwards and evokes the timber lined "stube" of the mountainous region to the north of Venice to create a cozy den in which to enjoy Pompei's renowned pizza. The reinvigorated Pompei's offers an exciting dining experience while placing a fresh scoop of Venice into Bondi's assorted sundae.

Nascha´s Denis Kosutic

Location: Vienna, Austria Floor Area: 100 sqm Completion Year: 2011 Photography: Lea Titz

On the way from a nostalgic Parisian bistro to a cool, New York-style deli, a mixture of strongly alienated classicistic details and pop art associated elements dominates the concept.

The broad product range has been atmospherically translated into the room design.

A colorful, placative, one of a kind wallpaper with animistic drawings embraces the room, forming a cheerful, ironic basis. In further steps, which have been applied as a branding in all corporate identity elements that have no connection to the room, the pattern becomes an essential element of the brand Nascha`s.

In a precise planning process, all product carriers have been reduced, in a functional manner, to the essential, while at the same time having been formed, in a very detailed manner. By doing so, a voluntary interpretation of the classic and well-known forms has been given priority. Colors have been reduced to black and white so as to draw attention to the gay world of colorful products in an optimal way.

A warm and not high-tech product illumination emphasizes a familiar atmosphere.

Adding vintage furniture and luminaire from the world of industry bestow upon the composition, which can be basically judged as elegant, a shabby chic touch, ensures surprising contrasts.

This makes the boundary between New and Old fade, with a playful timelessness being created.

The design developed in this manner has a nostalgic yet contemporary effect, being always on the borderline between irony and seriousness.

Gourmet Pastry 71 ARQUITECTOS

Location: Lisbon, Portugal **Floor Area:** 160 sqm **Completion Year:** 2011 **Photography:** João Morgado

For the gourmet pastry, 71 ARQUITECTOS have created a belt, disconnected from all the original structure, and all the elements, walls, ceilings and floors were painted matte black, leaving only the sight of the stone cladding of limestone of the arc that is presented in the lobby. The immaculate white belt surrounds all spaces, creating a relation between the various compartments, and at the same time allows to supporting any kind of decorative intervention by the customer. The belt allowed passing most of the infrastructures from behind, relying on the support structure of the belt, and avoiding the opening of rocky debris, thereby making the work faster and economical. All existing joinery was replaced by more slender steel profiles and without beams, allowing to establish a stronger link between the interior and the exterior.

The pastry develops from a wide entrance hall, divided by an arch. Perpendicular to the façade is the balcony of products on "Tiger Skin" limestone. In this room people can admire the exhibition of products, from the petit gateau to the colorful macaroons, served in the tea room on the left.

In the garden path people pass by the left side of the sanitary facilities, following the cafeteria and the respective counter also in "Tiger Skin". From the cafeteria people can see the garden / terrace which stretches itself over the botanical garden. The cafeteria area also accesses the laboratory / kitchen, the sanitary facilities for staff and the storage area.

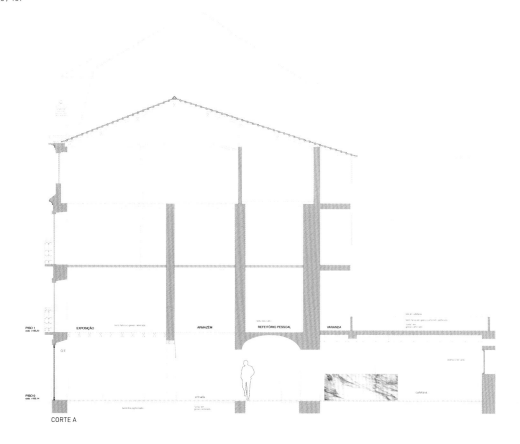

CORTE A

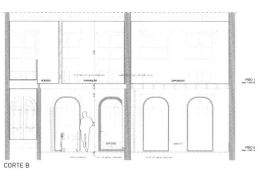

CORTE B

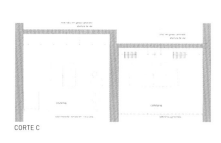

CORTE C

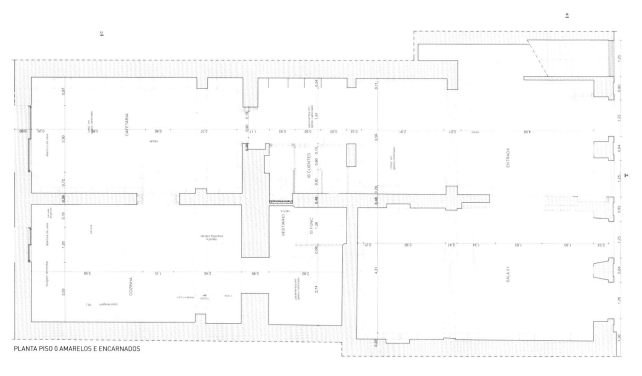

PLANTA PISO 0 AMARELOS E ENCARNADOS

Mr Tulk Projects of Imagination

Location: Melbourne, Australia **Floor Area:** 220 sqm **Completion Year:** 2007 **Photography:** Andrew Curtis, Renee Stamatis

Mr Tulk, a café set within the historic State Library of Victoria, plays extensively on the reading room vernacular. Its namesake, Augustus Henry Tulk was the library's first Chief Librarian and his silhouette plays a role in the interior. The long space with high ceilings is flooded with light from a succession of elegantly arched windows and is divided into two areas, one dining end, then the café, kitchen & take-out area at the other. The large communal table in the casual dining area is surrounded by bentwood chairs hand-dipped in red paint, bespoke blackened steel reading lights, and a customized vintage book wall & display cabinet. At the other end, copper clad bench-tops and bespoke display units define the take-out & bar area. The interior, encompassing huge, wall-mounted, anglepoise lamps, deep stained timber wall paneling, mixed Thonet furniture and intricate hand-drawn wall murals, makes you feel as if spreading out the newspaper is really valuable study.

Osteria BALLA Manfredi Luigi Rosselli Architects

Location: Sydney, Australia **Floor Area:** 600 sqm **Completion Year:** 2011 **Photography:** Justin Alexander

BALLA's kitchen and bar are raised up from the main floor level and are framed by concrete trusses referencing the bridges that span over the Milano's Navigli canal. Mild steel with visible weldings and fixings are used throughout the fitout referencing the past steel industry of Milano, and the wine storage is inspired by factory floor pigeon-hole racks.

The waterfront side of the restaurant has come to be known as "The Avenue". The Avenue is the connection between the inside of the restaurant and the larger waterfront landscape beyond the facade. Its rhythm is set by the large structural columns located inside the operable glazing facade.

The columns are important links between the internal landscape of the restaurant, and the natural harbourside landscape. The columns are architectural trees, clad with a modern floral mosaic tile, and branched with industrial Lingotto light fittings designed by Renzo Piano. Arranged in Futurist inspired geometry, the multi-colored ceiling panels above form a canopy of "foliage" and "sky".

Hand blown sculptural glass pendant lights by internationally acclaimed glass artist Dante Marioni hang from the ceiling adding a whimsical "feminine" glow to the otherwise masculine industrial fitout.

Luigi Rosselli has connected his childhood memories of the first "Futurist", Leonardo da Vinci's painted ceiling and walls of the Salla Delle Asse at Milan's Sforza Castle, and the Sydney landscape in a most unexpected combination.

Honest Entertainment has injected into the Southbank landscape a magical Chowpatty Beach pop-up bar and restaurant, named after the eponymous beach in Bombay for acclaimed restaurateurs Dishoom. Their design spirit and inspiration evolved from the discovery of a Hindi term "Jugaad" which means "making do", "reusing" or "creative improvisation".

Many of the materials are either recycled, found or secondhand and have been reinvented and up-cycled, creating a welcoming homely and relaxing vibe that is completely in keeping with the growing awareness and opportunity for sustainable design.

Tanya Clark, Creative Director at Honest Entertainment describes how "Dymo tags and clues can be found around the space telling the story of the origins of materials that have been re-fashioned. There is a wall constructed from tightly rolled newspapers, plastic bottles were recycled and pressed to make colorful psychedelic bar fascias, 'junk' rescued from skips and street corners has been recreated and loved to produce textural intrigue on the walls".

A patchwork of old freight pallets have been given a sunset scenic painted wash to create a unique stand-alone exterior cladding against the grey urban backdrop of the Queen Elizabeth Hall – At night the exterior glows and is transformed through intricate built-in lighting.

Dishoom Chowpatty Beach Honest Entertainment

Location: London, UK **Floor Area:** 177.9 sqm **Completion Year:** 2011 **Photography:** James Bedford & Sim Canetty-Clarke

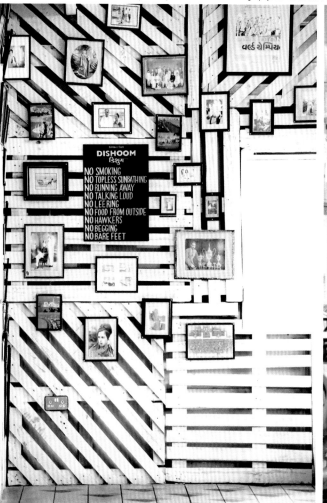

AREA A

AREA B

AREA C

DISHOOM PLAN EX FURNITURE V5

Casa Cor | Brastemp WHYDESIGN (Mauricio Arruda, Guto Requena, Tatiana Sakurai)

Location: São Paulo, Brazil **Floor Area:** 93 sqm **Completion Year:** 2010 **Photography:** Fran Parente

The kitchen is a functional space that hosts daily events and cooking classes. The entire space works as a real kitchen, with countertops, refrigerators, sinks and all necessary infrastructures. During two months of intense searching, designers gathered furniture, objects and hardware materials left behind in dumpsters around the city, or purchased them at extremely affordable prices at used furniture warehouses and stores in the neighborhood of Minhocão (Sao Paulo downtown) or at the Lar Escola São Francisco (not-for-profit thrift store). This concept can be immediately discerned at their front step, an assemblage of dumped doors found in those locations.

The entire floor is comprised of pallet boards, donated by CEAGESP (Sao Paulo's official farmer market), laid out in a classic fish scale design. The large kitchen countertop that provides support for the guests, chefs and their 25 students is a complex collage of eight granite countertops discarded in warehouses, which gain the status of cooking station designed to take advantage of the irregularity of the pieces. The result is a ready-made look that transmits an image of a giant centipede with industrial trestle legs that looks like it might walk in the space. All the hydraulic and electrical installations are visible and several ceramic vases with spices, peppers, kitchen utensils and organic waste containers compose the space.

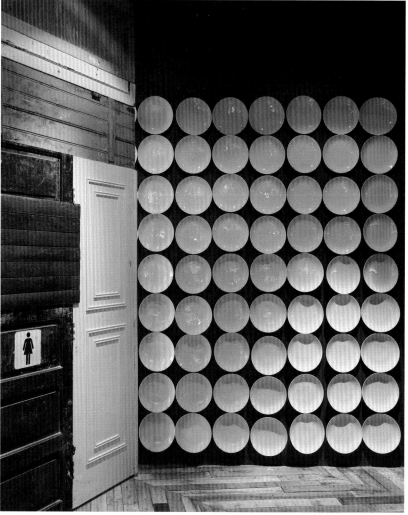

MOMO Restaurant, Bar and Lounge   Baranowitz Kronenberg Architects

Location: Amsterdam, the Netherlands   **Floor Area:** 350 sqm   **Completion Year:** 2008   **Photography:** Ewout Huibers

MOMO restaurant is located right in the middle of the bustling city center of Amsterdam, at the hub of the trendy and culturally stunning fashion and museum district. Situated on the historic and picturesque Singelgracht canal and taking its name from the Japanese meaning blossom and beauty.

MOMO is a fresh new venue to be experienced: an endless journey which has no set rules, but instead asks you to be creative and follow your own path.

The elegant fine-dining experience lives alongside a vibrant night-scene bar, which together create a luxurious melting pot for hotel guests, passing residents and tourists.

By using stainless steel in mirror finish panels, one can have an indirect view of the canal and the surrounding neighborhood. All tables and bar top are finished with glossy veneer that together with the mirror-finish panels to create a glamorous feel throughout the space. An open Asian-Fusion kitchen provides guests the exciting experience of watching the cooks and chefs with their energetic work.

Since its grand opening on October 2008, MOMO Restaurant, Bar and Lounge has been marked by the local press as the rising star of the gourmet and well-designed restaurants throughout the city.

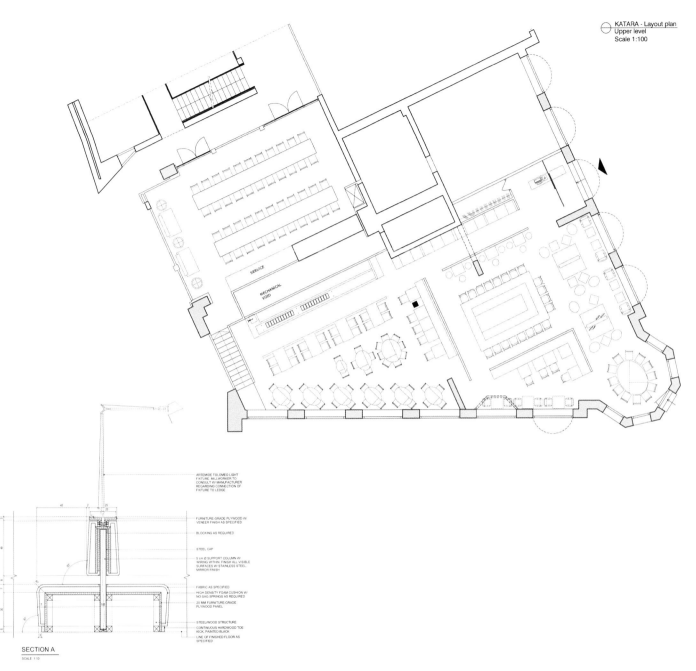

ARTEMIDE TOLOMEO LIGHT
FIXTURE. MILLWORKER TO
CONSULT W/ MANUFACTURER
REGARDING CONNECTION OF
FIXTURE TO LEDGE

FURNITURE-GRADE PLYWOOD W/
VENEER FINISH AS SPECIFIED

BLOCKING AS REQUIRED

STEEL CAP

5 cm Ø SUPPORT COLUMN W/
WIRING WITHIN. FINISH ALL VISIBLE
SURFACES W/ STAINLESS STEEL
MIRROR FINISH

FABRIC AS SPECIFIED

HIGH DENSITY FOAM CUSHION W/
NO SAG SPRINGS AS REQUIRED

20 MM FURNITURE-GRADE
PLYWOOD PANEL

STEEL/WOOD STRUCTURE

CONTINUOUS HARDWOOD TOE
KICK, PAINTED BLACK

LINE OF FINISHED FLOOR AS
SPECIFIED

SECTION A
SCALE 1:10

Lah! RESTAURANT ILMIODESIGN

Location: Madrid, Spain **Floor Area:** 350 sqm **Completion Year:** 2011 **Photography:** Usio Davila

PLANTA DISTRIBUCCION-Panel 1

LAH! Restaurant wants to win the challenge of introducing the South-East Asia through a new, innovative and unique space.

The project idea is to bring the core of a distant and unknown land with different cultures, customs and religions and shape it in a design which can produce a friendly space, speaking of architectural forms and proportions, to generate intense sensory emotions in the audience.

LAH! excites the visitor who is surprised to find a different place without the typical features of a Chinese or a Japanese restaurant. To achieve this aim, designers offer an unusual spatial distribution, thought as a continuous fragmentation of the main space, where vertical wood panels hung from the ceiling are opposed to those fastened to the floor and those leant against the walls. These panels remind people of those advertisements based on old images of huge Asian cities, where the apparent disorder generates in their mind the perception of an harmonious space, through the use of a fluid architectural language with a strong personality.

Beyond all doubt, these segmentations assure a pleasant experience in a comfortable environment composed of intimate spaces which turn out to be welcoming and stimulating to those using them.

Entering this restaurant, the customer realizes that LAH! is different from the rest!

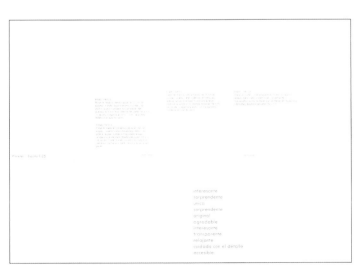

PANELES A-B-C-D-Panel 1

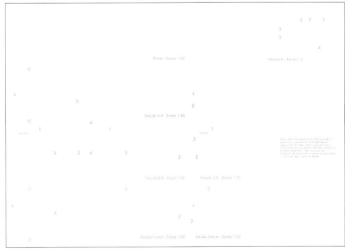

MESA GRANDE-Presentaci 1

Watermoon facet studio

Location: Sydney, Australia **Floor Area:** 120 sqm **Completion Year:** 2010 **Photography:** Katherine Lu

At the back streets of Kings Cross amongst restaurants and pubs, stands the old building which houses Watermoon.

The designers' task is to change the original tired pub with a history of over 15 years, to a restaurant which enables the enjoyment of Japanese cuisine alongside traditional sake. It was further requested by the client to communicate with people, even if they are looking up from the street, that Watermoon is a place where one can have both Japanese food and drink.

The characteristic of Japanese food, as represented by Sashimi, is to elaborate on the quality of raw material for a magical transformation to culinary art. From this they took clue to utilise the versatility of timber – which can be both structure and finish – all over the interior of Watermoon in various ways, to materialise the spirit of Japanese cuisine. By locating a lightbox at centre of the restaurant as a canvas to project colorful shadows of backlit sake bottles from within, its gentle illuminence brought out the prominence of timber in this space.

By backlighting sake bottles, which are approximately 1.3 times larger than wine bottles, their enlarged shadows are casted on a translucent membrane. The direct silhouette from the physical bottle and the virtual projection of its color and form, arouses curiosity as people ponder about the bottles in this stillness.

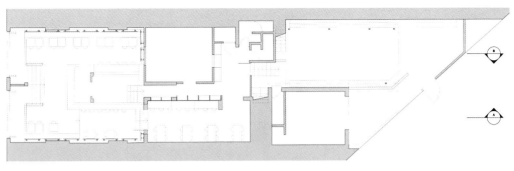

facet Water plan

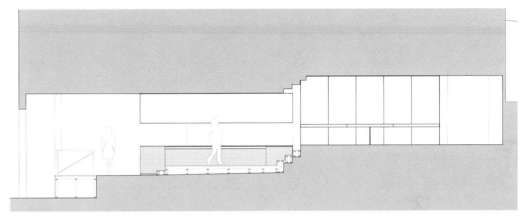

facet Water section A

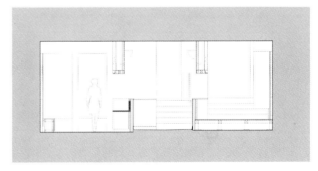

facet Water section D

Cafe in the Park Curiosity Inc.

Location: Osaka, Japan Floor Area: 256 sqm Completion Year: 2008 Photography: Nacasa & Partners

The space created around two large windows is a welcoming bright modern interior.

The "greige" (beige+grey) tone of the interior combined natural stones and washed wood, highlighted with a metallic sculptural lighting in the ceiling. A sense of modern luxury is created with the combination of lighting and materials. The contrast between the different zones, open space and intimate area create the ideal setting for the different customers.

In the center presented on large stones, a generous buffet is the highlight of the space, the special lighting will emphasize the color of the food on display.

The two floors open space in the back is the ideal space for all day dining, the metal sculpture on the ceiling becomes a strong lighting feature at night, reflected on the vertical grey glass wall.

Carefully designed flower arrangements are placed at different areas creating a dynamic and refined ambiance.

Clouds are used for the ceiling detail. There is IZUMO shrine, one of the most important shrines in Shimane Japan. The clouds people can see there, have a beautiful but mysterious image. SWeeT co.,Ltd wanted to show those images on the design of Tsujita LA.

The designer put 25,000 wooden sticks, which was shaped like drum stick on the ceiling.

In order to increase a reality of clouds, designer calculates the focal length between eye line and wooden sticks and uses that length for the stick length. Also he made difference on the distance between each stick so as to make a stereoscopic effect to the wooden cloud.

Not only for this project, the designer is always challenging to create a space in which art and interior coexist. At the same time, he'd like people to feel the delicacy of the Japanese beauty, and the Japanese atmosphere that when people visit here, they will want to visit Japan. He'd like to make this restaurant as one of the elements.

Tsujita LA SWeeT co.,Ltd

Location: Los Angeles, USA **Floor Area:** 70 sqm **Completion Year:** 2011 **Photography:** Nacasa & Partners Inc

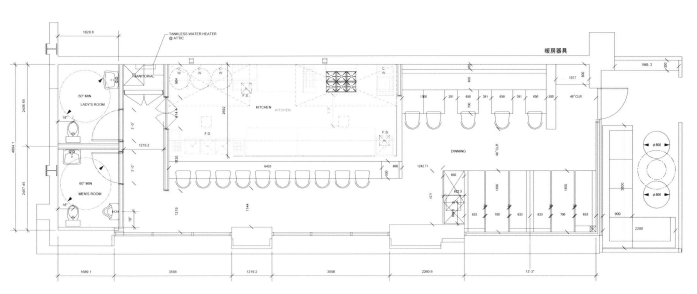

Sofa: 5 table 10seats
Booth: 2table 12seats
Counter: 10seats

Omonia Bakery bluarch architecture + interiors + lighting

Location: New York, USA **Floor Area:** 1,480 sq ft **Completion Year:** 2011 **Photography:** ADO, Scott G Morris Photography

This bakery is a brand new project for the family behind the renowned Omonia brand famous for its Greek pastries. It sells pastries and bread prepared on premises in the see-through kitchen.

The design of this store celebrates indulgence – the suspension of one's everyday grind through the consumption of a sweet delight. The space is soft and warm, sexy and decadent, like chocolate.

Much like the physiognomy of a pastry, this design wants to offer the exciting anticipation of a pastry in-fieri, the liquid concoction and the minced ingredients. The space shifts organically with the narrative of flavors as patrons taste the succulent goods.

The main feature of the 1,000sf interior space is a fluid surface (clad with ¼" chocolate brown Bisazza tiles) which covers the ceiling and the side walls to different heights. This surface warps in bubbles and negotiates a system of 6-inch tubular incandescent light bulbs and an arrangement of red cedar wood spheres. The epoxy flooring continues to the walls via filleted corners. A shelf and LED strips navigate the transition with the chocolate surface.

The kitchen is exhibited to the public, as it sits simply within a tempered glass box. Therefore, the exquisite level of craftsmanship of the project, with its unforgiving alignments and complex details, is paralleled with the refined artisanship of Omonia's pastries.

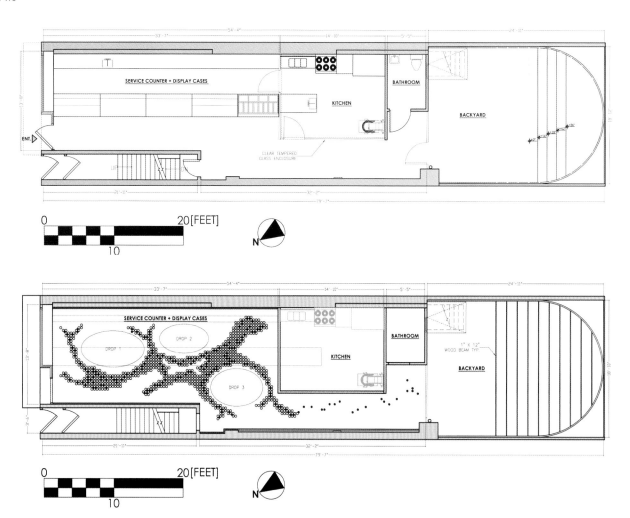

SERVICE COUNTER + DISPLAY CASES

KITCHEN

BATHROOM

BACKYARD

ENT.

UP

CLEAR TEMPERED
GLASS ENCLOSURE

0   10   20 [FEET]

N

SERVICE COUNTER + DISPLAY CASES

DROP 1

DROP 2

DROP 3

KITCHEN

BATHROOM

BACKYARD

1" X 12"
WOOD BEAM TYP.

0   10   20 [FEET]

N

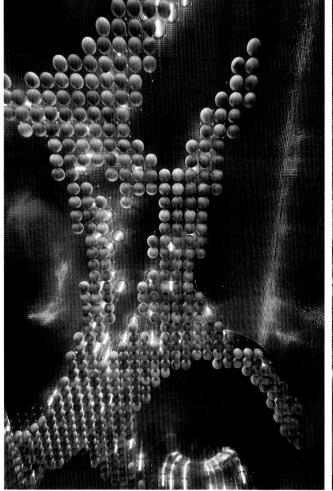

Vyta Boulangerie Italiana COLLIDANIELARCHITETTO

Location: Turin, Italy **Floor Area:** 150 sqm **Completion Year:** 2011 **Photography:** Matteo Piazza

La Natura offre elementi
semplici: acqua, grano e fuoco.
La mano esperta, la pazienza
e la creatività dell'uomo creano
da millenni forme, sapori
e profumi fragranti:
il pane alimentazione
dell'umanità antica e moderna

The project features contrasting materials and colors: oak and Corian as representatives of tradition and innovation, an integration of nature and artifice. The juxtaposition of soft oak and black declined in its various material aspects creates an exclusive, theatrical environment, where the warmth of the natural texture is enhanced by the contrast with glossy black surfaces and volumes. These come up as large ceramic tiles on the floor, Corian for the counter and black polymer for all the vertical panels that fold the space like in a treasure chest.

"Through simple products offered by Nature, such as water, wheat and fire, thanks to Man's expert hand, patience and creativity, forms, savors and fragrant flavors have been created for millennia, giving birth to bread, ancient and modern nourishment for manhood." This food philosophy was the starting point that inspired the architectural concept.

A contemporary look has been reformulated for the most "minimal" product on tables. It originates from a restraint design and an innovative, cool elegance, the result being a sophisticated minimalism and a formal reduction to the essential.

The hexagonal tables are custom-designed into a shape and distribution that refer to the pure geometry of bee-hives. At the same time the ensemble evokes the ancient rite of eating together, a less common practice nowadays, but increasingly necessary in the third millennium's life.

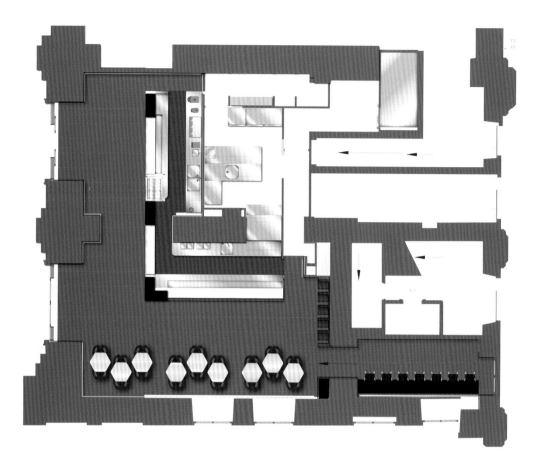

Plan

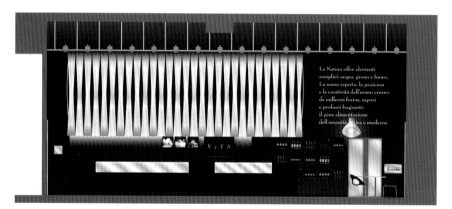

Cross Section

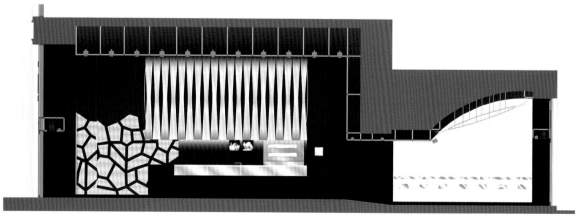

Longitudinal Section

Maximiliano FreelandBuck

Location: Los Angeles, USA **Floor Area:** 2,750 sq ft **Completion Year:** 2011 **Photography:** Nils Timm

Maximiliano is an Italian restaurant and pizzeria for chef Andre Guerrero that opened in October 2011 in Los Angeles. The 2,200 square-foot tenant improvement is atmospherically distinct; a unique triangular dining area infused with color and evocative of the rich and refined menu. A large mural on the large south wall creates a strong graphic and spatial identity, evoking the rhythmic yet varied shapes of Guerrero's handmade pastas. The rhythm of embossed white stripes shifts from evenly parallel at the ceiling to randomly wavy at the seats, giving a gravitational weight to the wall and infusing the space with vibrant color and pattern. Descending over a door to the patio is a deep porous soffit that undulates over the bar, filtering natural and artificial light and housing the restaurant's wine collection. The brightly painted slats animate the space with local and varied color intensities creating 3D optical effects as the viewer moves that recall the visual instability of 1970's Op Art.

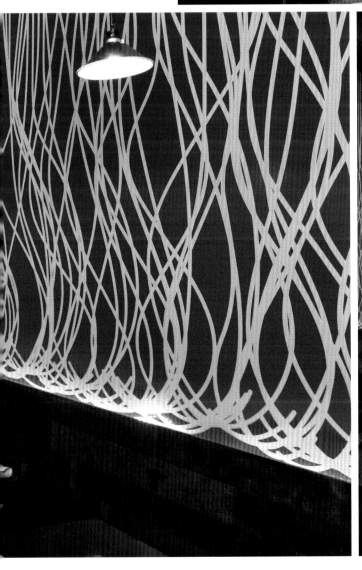

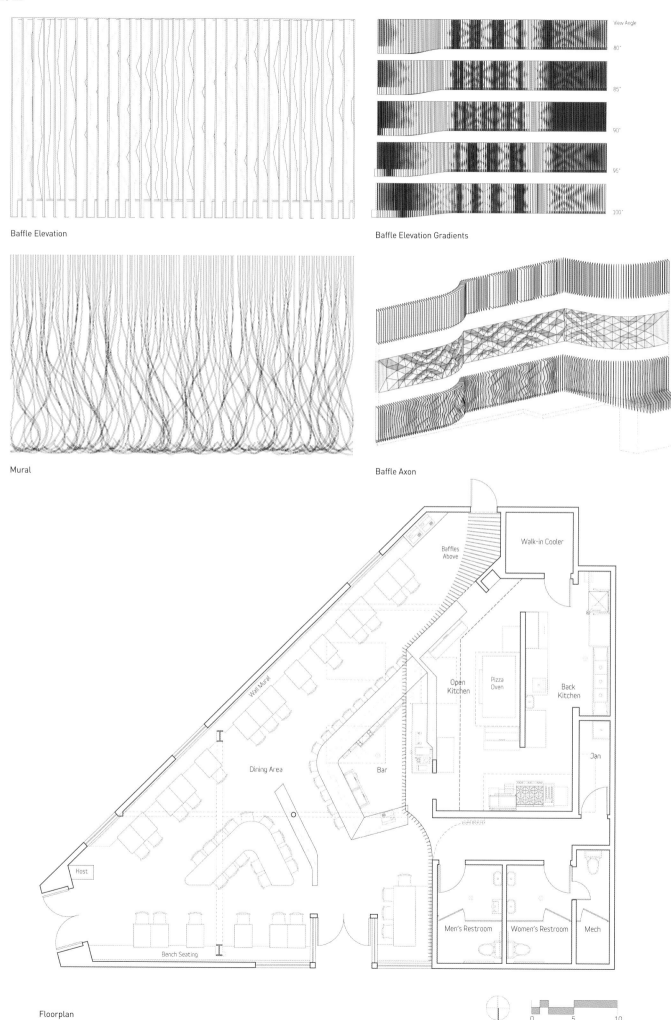

Baffle Elevation

Baffle Elevation Gradients

View Angle

80°

85°

90°

95°

100°

Mural

Baffle Axon

Undulating F

Trim Surface

Light Baffle & Soffit

Walk-in Cooler

Baffles Above

Open Kitchen

Pizza Oven

Back Kitchen

Jan

Bar

Wall Mural

Dining Area

Host

Men's Restroom

Women's Restroom

Mech

Bench Seating

Floorplan

N

0   5   10

FUEL Café at Chesapeake Elliott + Associates Architects

Location: Oklahoma City, USA **Floor Area:** 3,821 sq ft **Completion Year:** 2008 **Photography:** Scott McDonald, Hedrich Blessing

Hip and high energy are the key words here. The team started out with a bland, 4,000-square-foot space that used to house Chesapeake's accounting department. It had natural light on three sides, but that was it for visual excitement. The ceilings were low, the floors gray, and the general atmosphere gloomy. The architects gutted it to create a clean, white space, essentially a large reflector, to which they added T8 fluorescents with color gels, LED lamps, and laminated-glass panels with polyester film. There are no computers, fancy fixtures, or any sophisticated dimmers. Yet from this bare-bones technology comes a stunning range of intense color that complements the food being served: banana yellow and chili-pepper red, the cool pink of watermelon, and the deep purple of eggplant. The cooking island in the center of the restaurant is covered in red and green resin panels, like a floating Italian salad.

FUEL celebrates the interplay of color and daylight, with color being a starting point and first principle for the architect instead of a decorative afterthought.

The café has as many moods as the day: soft and welcoming in the morning, bright and upbeat at lunch, subdued in the late afternoon. The light is multidirectional as it streams through laminated-glass panels, bounces off walls and floors, and zips across ceilings in vibrant fluorescent stripes. Even mechanical chases are light sources. The glowing rectangular boxes at opposite ends of the café, with their green and blue LED lights, hide the exhausts from the prep kitchen below. Everywhere colors intersect and overlap, turning the interior into a Fauve painting.

Tori Tori Restaurant rojkind arquitectos, Esrawe Studio

Location: Mexico City, Mexico **Floor Area:** 629 sqm **Completion Year:** 2011 **Photography:** Paúl Rivera

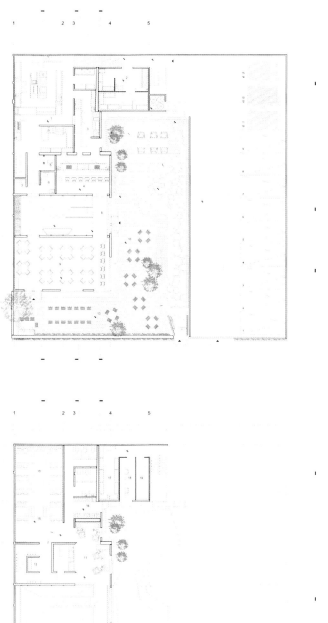

1- KITCHEN
2- REFRIGERATION CHAMBERS
3- SUSHI KITCHEN
4- SUSHI BAR
5- CASHIER
6- HANDICAP RESTROOM
7- WARDROBE
8- RECEPTION AREA
9- RESTAURANT
10- TERRACE
11- BAR
12- RESTAURANT

13- SERVICE AREA
14- RESTROOMS
15- TEA ROOM
16- TEA ROOM'S TERRACE
17- STORAGE
18- ADMINISTRATION AREA
19- LOCKERS
20- EMPLOYEES' RESTROOM (ME
21- EMPLOYEES' RESTROOM (W
22- LAUNDRY
23- EMPLOYEES' DINING ROOM

TORI TORI
FIRST FLOOR PLAN

1- KITCHEN
2- REFRIGERATION CHAMBERS
3- SUSHI KITCHEN
4- SUSHI BAR
5- CASHIER
6- HANDICAP RESTROOM
7- WARDROBE
8- RECEPTION AREA
9- RESTAURANT
10- TERRACE
11- BAR
12- RESTAURANT

13- SERVICE AREA
14- RESTROOMS
15- TEA ROOM
16- TEA ROOM'S TERRACE
17- STORAGE
18- ADMINISTRATION AREA
19- LOCKERS
20- EMPLOYEES' RESTROOM (MEN)
21- EMPLOYEES' RESTROOM (WOMEN)
22- LAUNDRY
23- EMPLOYEES' DINING ROOM

TORI TORI
SECOND FLOOR PLAN

1- KITCHEN
2- REFRIGERATION CHAMBERS
3- SUSHI KITCHEN
4- SUSHI BAR
5- CASHIER
6- HANDICAP RESTROOM
7- WARDROBE
8- RECEPTION AREA
9- RESTAURANT
10- TERRACE
11- BAR
12- RESTAURANT

13- SERVICE AREA
14- RESTROOMS
15- TEA ROOM
16- TEA ROOM'S TERRACE
17- STORAGE
18- ADMINISTRATION AREA
19- LOCKERS
20- EMPLOYEES' RESTROOM (MEN)
21- EMPLOYEES' RESTROOM (WOMEN)
22- LAUNDRY
23- EMPLOYEES' DINING ROOM

TORI TORI
THIRD FLOOR PLAN

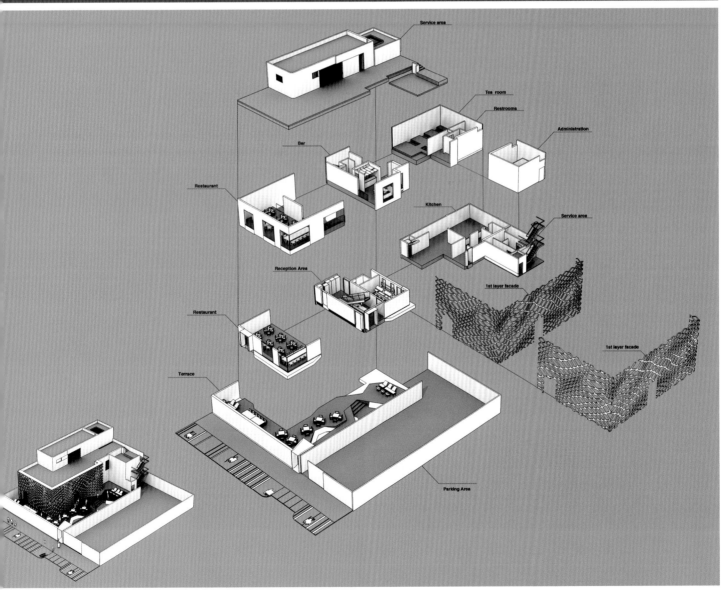

Considered one of the best Japanese restaurants in Mexico City and due to its remarkable success, Tori Tori has now moved to a bigger location in the same area of Polanco, Mexico City, where rojkind arquitectos and Esrawe Studio teamed up to make it happen.

Maintaining a very intimate and subtle feel towards the first encounter with the exterior, once you enter you'll find yourself in a terrace, where eating and drinking are embraced by natural vegetation. The building's organic façade and landscape were carefully designed to become an extension of the restaurant, creating a strong relationship between the inside and the outside.

The interior receives and follows the exterior with subtle contrasts. Each room has its own nature and shows a clear relationship with its function. The furniture was inspired and made for Tori Tori and developed with a direct orientation through each space. During more than eight months a complete collection of chairs and tables were created, for both exterior and interior.

The façade, which seems to emerge from the ground climbing up through the building, as if mimicking the natural ivy surrounding the retaining walls, is made up of two self-supporting layers of steel plates cut with a CNC machine and handcrafted to exact specifications.

The façade's pattern responds to the openings inside, filtering light, shadows, and views that will constantly invade the interior spaces. It is an atmosphere enriched by the spectrum of subtle changes.

ZOZOBRA Asian Noodle Bar offers a dynamic eating experience through fast service, supported by energetic staff and a sizzling state of the artistic open kitchen. Here, private territory is blurred. The use of communal dining arrangement encourages guests to approach each other, while the ever-changing LED lighting schemes and the video art on walls enhance the interaction with ZOZOBRA's world.

The ambiance is a mix of the rigorous design approach and the energetic, pop atmosphere of a fast service restaurant. The world represented on the video art takes clients on an emotional and imaginary journey away from their daily life. The open kitchen is the heart of ZOZOBRA: it radiates the energies which burst from its tops, wok pans and stoves. The kitchen is wrapped by a three-dimensional origami structure: a binging element between the culinary world of ZOZOBRA and its stimulating personality.

The mirrored black ceiling amplifies and reflects what happens on the floor. The black table tops are perfect background for the ecstatic dishes while the white surfaces are the perfect setting for displaying the heart and soul of ZOZOBRA.

ZOZOBRA Asian Noodle Bar Baranowitz Kronenberg Architects

Location: Kfar-Sabba, Israel **Floor Area:** 550 sqm **Completion Year:** 2011 **Photography:** Amit Geron

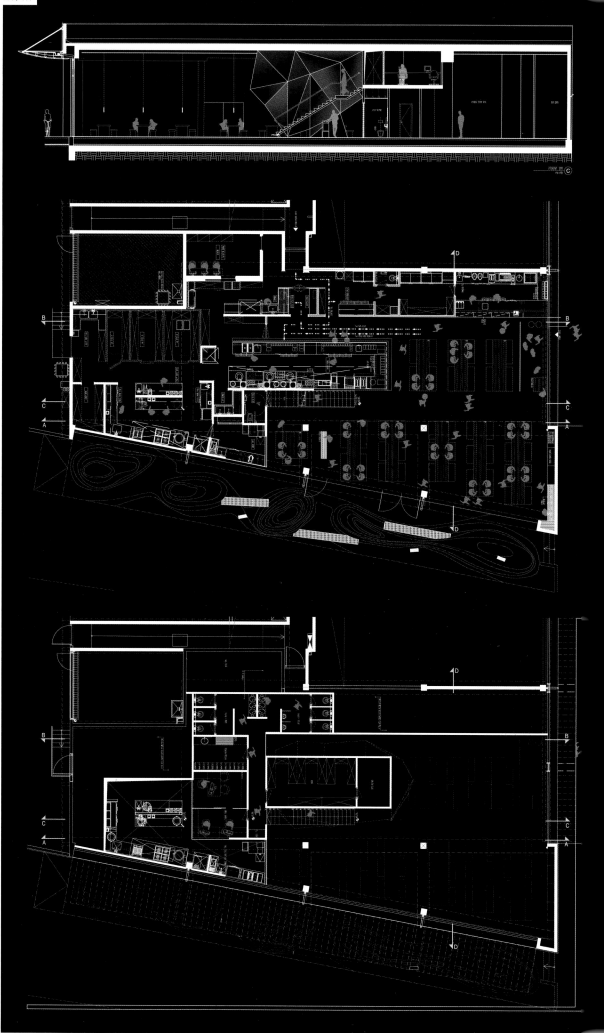

Monvínic Alfons Tost Interiorisme

Location: Barcelona, Spain **Floor Area:** 500 sqm **Completion Year:** 2008 **Photography:** Eugeni Pons

It was important to show the culture of the wine, for that the desigenrs opt to escape from the commercial spaces. It was also important to create a space where they can transmit the meaning of the wine in the interior.

They want to obtain that the clients of Monvinic sees the space as liquid. The first contact of the space had to be directly with the culture, that's why they create firstly an emblematic space, the library, which is the connection between wine and culture.

Through the corridor they are finding places where people can sit. They created the wine bar, where people begin to get contact physically and directly with the wine. Here is where the main concept of the project was born, the wine cellar, set behind cinnamon transparent glass.

Going up 3 steps there finds the gastronomic space – the wine tasting space. On the wall there is the menu, and behind it, the entrance to the kitchen and the bathrooms.

To go through the last glass sheet people enter the tasting room, where they hold all the courses, tasting and conference. One table for the teacher with his own washstand reminds us of a laboratory with technology and sensibility.

At the bottom, the exterior space presides at 3 totems with lids, where people can enjoy smoking cigarettes while they are reading texts about Monvínic music – JAZZ.

Café 501 Elliott + Associates Architects

Location: Oklahoma, USA **Floor Area:** 5,400 sq ft **Completion Year:** 2010 **Photography:** Scott McDonald, Hedrich Blessing

The design was for the new construction of a 5,400 square feet space with dining area for 120 and a bar for 15. There is no private dining. The super-efficient kitchen has a wood-fired oven. The mezzanine provides space for an office and storage.

Key points from a discussion session with the client included the idea of fresh, local, fast, casual service at lunch. Café 501 would have a different atmosphere at night with a full service menu and staff. To maintain the owners' standards from the Boulevard Steakhouse, the focus is on quality food.

Café 501 incorporates the theme in the form of a "neighborhood café." At Classen Curve it will be comparable to the Edmond location, similar but not exact. The interior is wood, brick, steel, and glass with an open kitchen that is warm and friendly. The materials surrounding the guests include the woven, wood, ceramics, rope, stone and leather.

The materials created by hand are hewn, tanned, knitted, tied and textured. The "design recipe" is food and atmosphere that are woven together and handmade. The food and space are natural, fresh and authentic. There is blended space and woven light. Café 501 has two moods: in daytime when it is open, light in weight, natural atmosphere, and with an open kitchen; and in the evening there is a warm glow, firelight, shadows and drama, with an intimate setting. The design brings in the earth, sun, moon, stars and planets; most of all, it is a personal space.

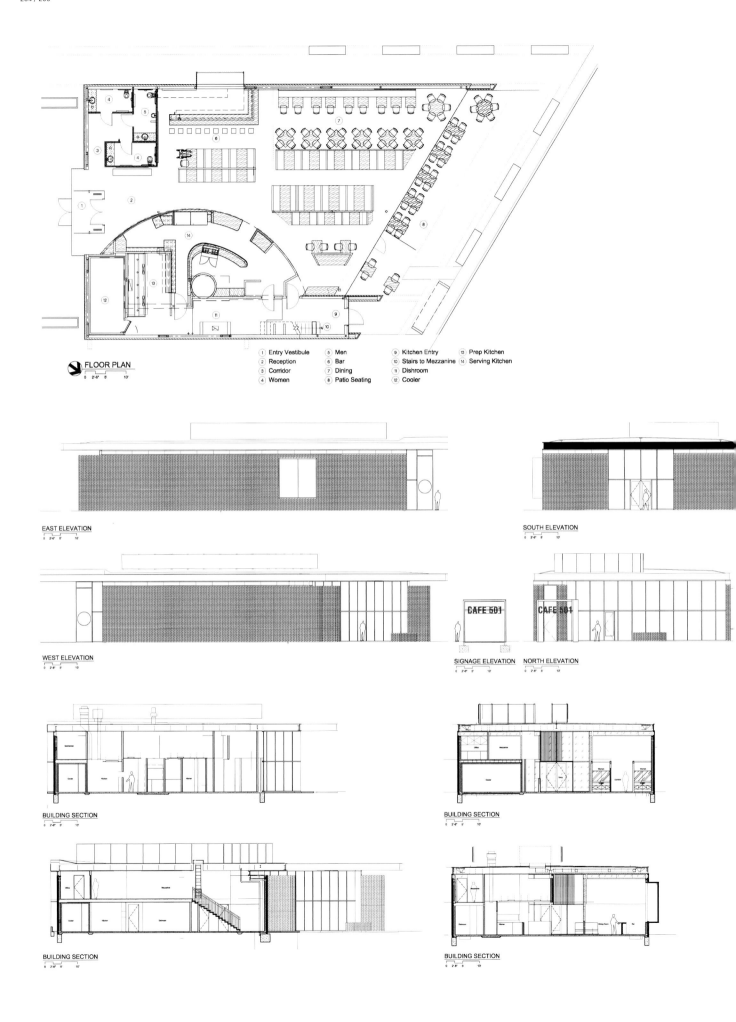

FLOOR PLAN

1 Entry Vestibule   5 Men   9 Kitchen Entry   13 Prep Kitchen
2 Reception   6 Bar   10 Stairs to Mezzanine   14 Serving Kitchen
3 Corridor   7 Dining   11 Dishroom
4 Women   8 Patio Seating   12 Cooler

EAST ELEVATION

SOUTH ELEVATION

WEST ELEVATION

SIGNAGE ELEVATION   NORTH ELEVATION

BUILDING SECTION

BUILDING SECTION

BUILDING SECTION

BUILDING SECTION

ELEMENTS at Chesapeake Elliott + Associates Architects

Location: Oklahoma, USA **Floor Area:** 11,040 sq ft **Completion Year:** 2009 **Photography:** Scott McDonald, Hedrich Blessing

ELEMENTS Restaurant responds to the potential customers and available space. The concept introduces an organic, natural, and inviting atmosphere using wood. It has a warm glow and a few surprises mixed in. The goal is to "shape the light" and fill the space with natural sunlight, shade and shadow. There is texture created using rift-cut white oak with a medium-brown stain. It features an elegant and comfortable "spa" menu. For the exterior, a 4-story steel sunshade was created to control the sun from south and west and to add detail and human scale to a 1980s precast concrete box.

When creating the architectural concept there were existing conditions to consider. The other three Chesapeake corporate campus restaurants were each designed with a specific concept. The Wildcat Restaurant includes stone and rustic surfaces featuring home cooking. The Chesapeake Conservatory is a light and airy space with high-performance glass to create a transparent structure. It has the feel of a garden room along the creek which allows an outdoor experience. FUEL Café is a colorful and high energy space with a "kitchen as art" concept. At FUEL colored glass on the perimeter window paints the space with soft color.

The menu options consist of healthy and light food selections which cater to the modern lifestyle. The exhibition kitchen allows the diners to view the food as it is prepared. The restaurant also offers a "to go" option.

1. Entry
2. Lobby/Reception
3. Conference
4. Women
5. Men
6. A/V Room
7. Elevator Lobby
8. Stair
9. Elec./Fire Pump
10. Corridor
11. Stair
12. Ramp
13. Elevated Dining
14. Main Dining
15. South Patio Dining
16. West Patio Dining
17. Checkout
18. Serving Line
19. Cookline
20. Kitchen
21. Mechanical Room
22. Walk-in Cooler
23. Service Entry
24. Service Entry Court
25. Janitor Closet
26. Dry Storage
27. Not in Scope of Project

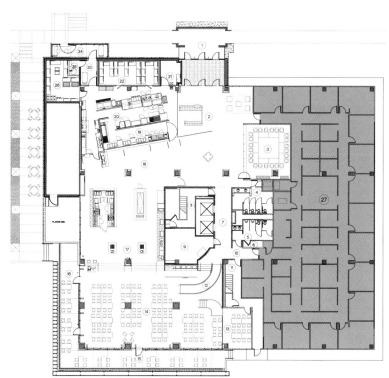

GROUND LEVEL FLOOR PLAN

0   7'-6"   15'   30'

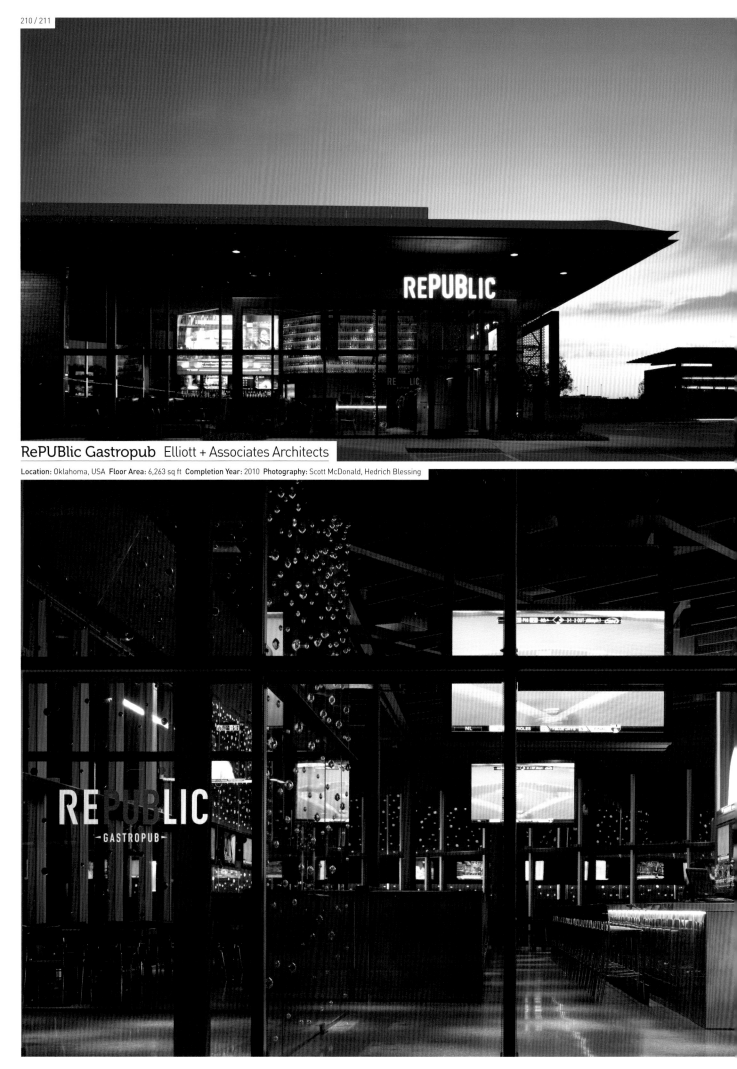

RePUBlic Gastropub Elliott + Associates Architects

Location: Oklahoma, USA **Floor Area:** 6,263 sq ft **Completion Year:** 2010 **Photography:** Scott McDonald, Hedrich Blessing

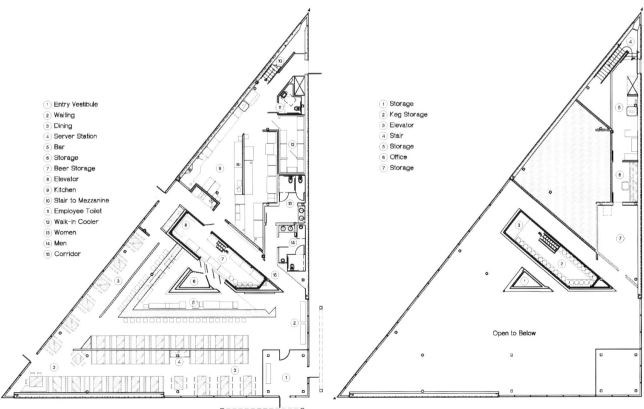

First Floor Plan	Mezzanine Floor Plan
1. Entry Vestibule	1. Storage
2. Waiting	2. Keg Storage
3. Dining	3. Elevator
4. Server Station	4. Stair
5. Bar	5. Storage
6. Storage	6. Office
7. Beer Storage	7. Storage
8. Elevator	
9. Kitchen	
10. Stair to Mezzanine	
11. Employee Toilet	
12. Walk-in Cooler	
13. Women	
14. Men	
15. Corridor	

FIRST FLOOR PLAN

0 5 10 20'

MEZZANINE FLOOR PLAN

0 5 10 20'

The architects' approach to the design supports the proposed name, menu, and spirit of the project concept, which is developed around the "spirit of sport."

There is power and grace, and strong muscular qualities. It is a place with spectacle where you can cheer your team on with all your friends, a place for a comfortable, memorable dinner with signature food and beverage. It will be a great place to hang out.

Central focus is a 200" projection screen and 103" plasmas with 42" eye level LCDs for bar patrons. There are 2-story beer cooler and beer bottle display, bar for 30 patrons, bubble wall, seating for 171 - 88 in booths and 53 at tables and chairs, seating for 16 on the outdoor patio, as an outdoor room with 4 plasma TVs and fans built-in to the TV enclosure. Eight foot Nellie Stevens hedge provides a sun and wind break and makes the patio more of a surprise for patrons.

Booths are made of paperstone with coarse leather seats and white oak wood tables. The floor uses dark grey marble terrazzo with a dark grey matrix. Ceiling is painted with exposed steel structure and metal deck with suspended sound panels. Bar was copper, top and face, with a steel plate footrest and soft downlight from underneath. South accent wall is the bubble wall. Separation walls at bar, booths and kitchen wall are paperstone. There is multi-color LED lighting from corridor to toilets.

Coral Restaurant Duarte Caldeira

Location: Madeira, Portugal **Floor Area:** 530 sqm **Completion Year:** 2009 **Photography:** Fernando Guerra / FG+SG

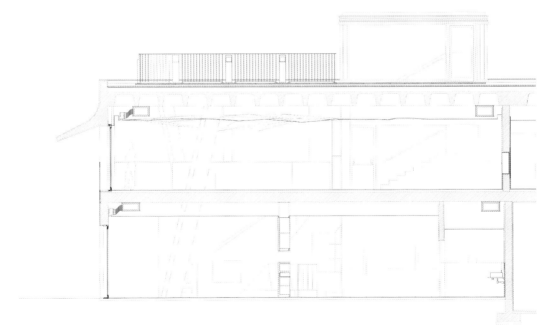

section BB

Coral is a restaurant located in a picturesque fishing village in Madeira Island.

When the designers created the project for an urban renewal of the area, the old restaurant was demolished and replaced by a new one in the same spot.

The site is on the seafront with spectacular views of the Atlantic Ocean, the surrounding cliffs and mountains. People can also watch fabulous sunsets.

The restaurant has two floors, one terrace and one large balcony. The terrace is by the entrance floor in the piazza, and the balcony is on the second floor.

The interior of the restaurant is in black and white – black granite on the floors, and white marble, plaster and paint on the walls. The color scheme matches the deep seawater black scabbard fish, Madeira's most known capture. Under its shinny black skin, you find a delicate and delicious white meat.

Wall-size photographs portraying the village's history and its profound relationship with the sea, were taken by a local photographer in the 1960s, bringing the local culture and atmosphere to the restaurant.

Between the ground floor and the first floor, there is a void which allows the visitor to look up at the silver ceiling. The reflections made by its irregular pleated surface give people the impression of being underwater.

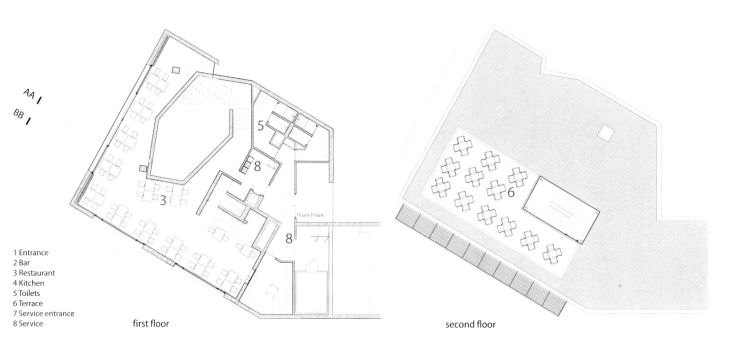

AA
BB

1 Entrance
2 Bar
3 Restaurant
4 Kitchen
5 Toilets
6 Terrace
7 Service entrance
8 Service

first floor

second floor

LLUÇANÈS RESTAURANT Josep Ferrando

Location: Barcelona, Spain **Floor Area:** 500 sqm **Completion Year:** 2008 **Photography:** Adrià Goula

The space is divided between the two existing plants, on the ground floor more informal, and at the top, a Michelin Star restaurant.

The ground floor space is as a continuum of the square, with a large opening at front and a continuous concrete floor, becoming a door between the public space and the market. The layout creates two working parties on both sides: one open, where the layout of the kitchens in perpendicular encourages people to watch the show, and one close to the dirty area with access from the outside service. Lighting along the place reinforces the idea of continuity, turning the square into a restaurant and plaza.

The first floor is achieved by a great cabinet space; positioned asymmetrically in the room, creates four places between the perimeter of the facades, so that the container and metal beams are continuously deployed. The floor, with references to aerial photographs of the fields, indicates the importance of raw material in a restaurant, while carpets generate three intensities of gray that individualize each table.

The material of the proposal seeks to maintain the industrial character of the market, using steel plates and concrete.

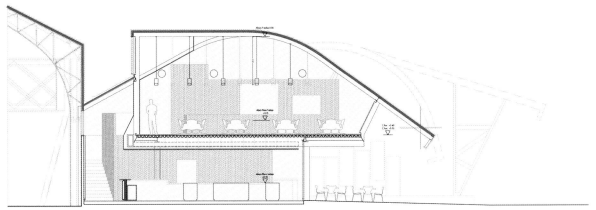

SECCIÓN AA' E: 1/150

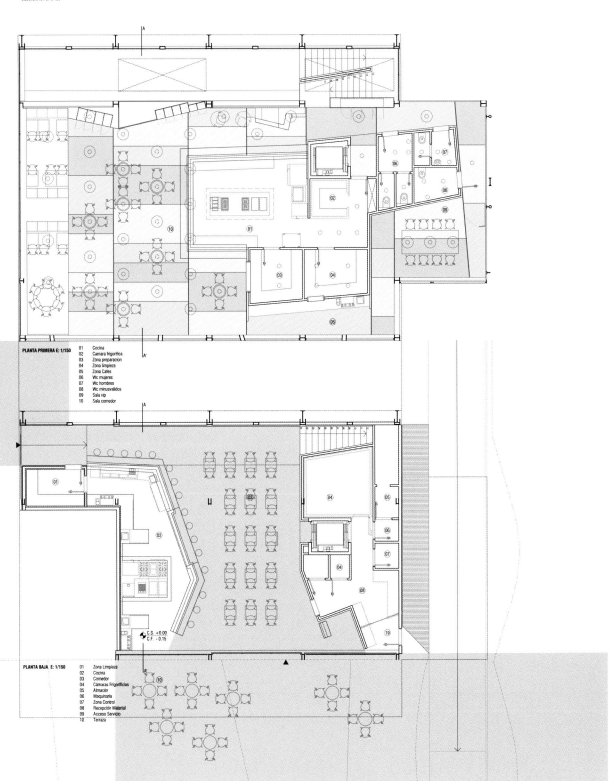

PLANTA PRIMERA E: 1/150

01	Cocina
02	Camara frigorifica
03	Zona preparacion
04	Zona limpieza
05	Zona Cafes
06	Wc mujeres
07	Wc hombres
08	Wc minusvalidos
09	Sala vip
10	Sala comedor

PLANTA BAJA E: 1/150

01	Zona Limpieza
02	Cocina
03	Comedor
04	Cámaras Frigorificas
05	Almacén
06	Maquinaria
07	Zona Control
08	Recepción Material
09	Acceso Servicio
10	Terraza

C.S. +0.00
C.F. - 0.15

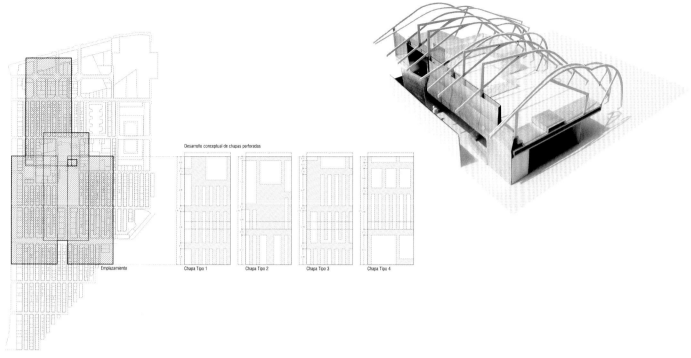

Desarrollo conceptual de chapas perforadas

Emplazamiento

Chapa Tipo 1
Chapa Tipo 2
Chapa Tipo 3
Chapa Tipo 4

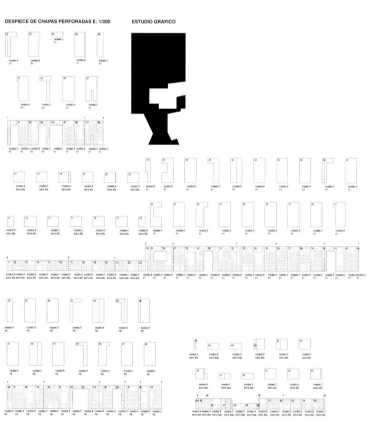

DESPIECE DE CHAPAS PERFORADAS E: 1/200

ESTUDIO GRAFICO

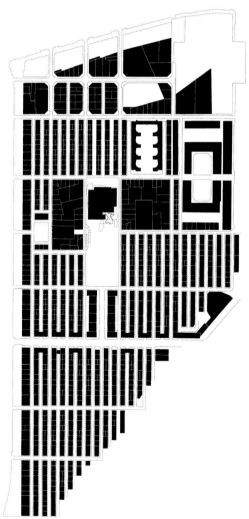

SECCIÓN BARRAS TIPO   E : 1/20

MATERIALES:
- Tochana cerámica 9.14.28
- Chapa de acero plegada en bandeja y perforada sujeta a montantes verticales de acero galvani. 80.40.3, acabada en pátina de color blanco
- Lámina textil microperforada, acabada en colo
- Pletina corrida de acero de 150.5 de espesor, pátina blanca
- Pletina L.150.40.5
- Iluminación de tipo fluorescente sujeta a pletin 120.40.5, apoyada sobre montantes verticales
- Vidrio corrido tintado en negro
- Perfil T.45.45.5

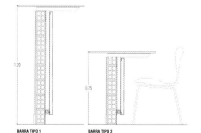

BARRA TIPO 1   BARRA TIPO 2

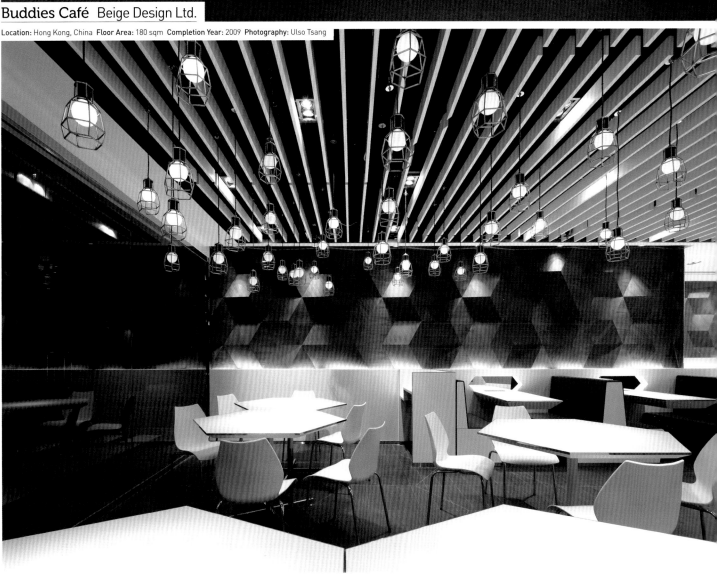

Buddies Café Beige Design Ltd.

Location: Hong Kong, China **Floor Area:** 180 sqm **Completion Year:** 2009 **Photography:** Ulso Tsang

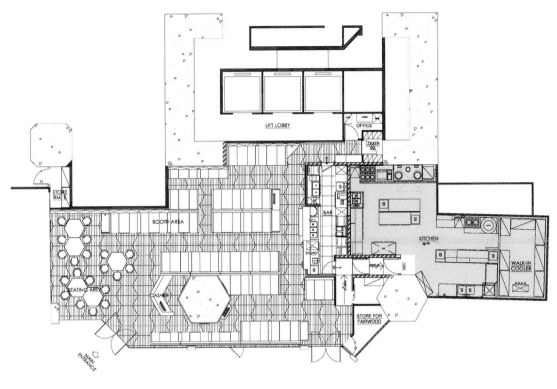

FURNITURE LAYOUT PLAN 1 : 50

PROPOSED LAYOUT SEATING CAPACITY:
105 PERSONS

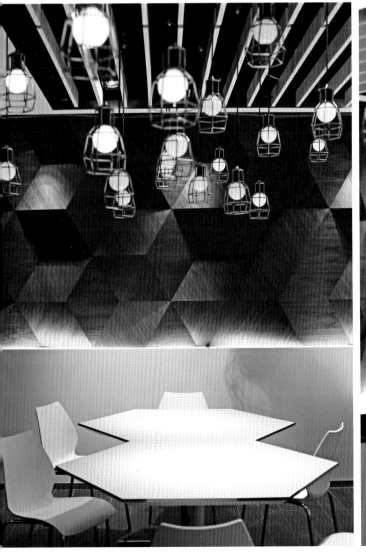

Inspired by a huge hexagonal column in the floor plan, this delicate design was sparked off with the geometry chic and being resonated throughout the space. Taking a two-dimension concept, the geometric form develops it into a three-dimensional interior architectural perspective with innovations and explorations.

A pristine reception counter made with Corian® marks a fascinating welcome. Subtlety of the design can be traced from the diamond-cut hexagonal Corian® sculptural counters.

The loosing hexagonal seating area can be transformed to be a honeycomb to cater for flexible buddies' gatherings. While there are subtle lines dividing the ceiling blocks into hexagonal zones, the suspension light bulbs are also wired with polygon-shaped motifs in a loose hexagonal arrangement.

The stunning effect of the illusion is magnified by the hundreds of hexagons hidden in the three-layered staggered woodcraft panels in lights and shades.

Relax at the booth seating, you will find the intimacy of space from the details of the inclined table edges and table-end mirror.

The giant hexagonal column which inspired the whole concept is at last disappeared. These mirrors lead to strong reflections on the hexagonal cells in the space to multiply the effect of uniqueness and consistency.

Der SPIEGEL canteen Ippolito Fleitz Group

Location: Hamburg, Germany **Floor Area:** 525 sqm **Completion Year:** 2011 **Photography:** Zooey Braun

Despite the size of the space the visitor should never have an impression of monotonous, interchangeable, production-line construction. Rather the goal is to illustrate, in a dining context, the culture of dialogue which has flourished over the decades at SPIEGEL. The employees' canteen is a meeting place, a place of culture and informal exchange of opinions. At the same time it should fulfil functional obligations such as accessibility and spatial clarity.

The round, communicative tables are made from black coated steel frames which seem to grow from the floor in a graceful motion. Granite plates serve as table tops, their lasered surfaces working with the ceiling lights to create glare-free, brilliant light. The tables are placed within the space in three large groups in loose arrangements and so provide an organic counterpoint to the polygonal floor plan. Movement zones are thus clearly delineated. Three lines are set into the smooth, white terrazzo floor: they ensure tables don't encroach on walkways. Along these lines four areas are arranged with removable, lightweight spatial filters composed of white, hanging rods. Large yellow light dishes support the zoning of the space just as the hanging lamps locating tables within the space.

Wood panelling lends a sense of depth to structural hubs. The whitewashed, varnished surfaces appear even deeper thanks to a vertical, wavy relief which gives a textile-like effect.

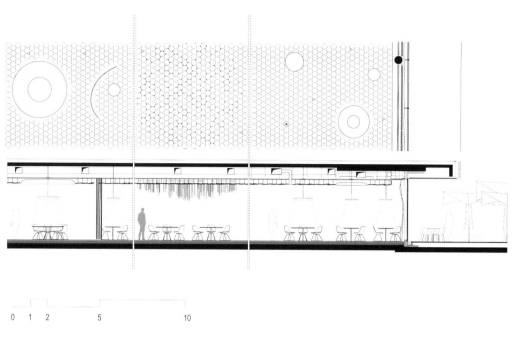

0 1 2   5   10

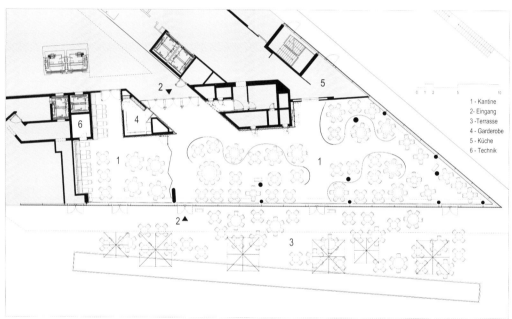

0 1 2   5   10

1 - Kantine
2 - Eingang
3 - Terrasse
4 - Garderobe
5 - Küche
6 - Technik

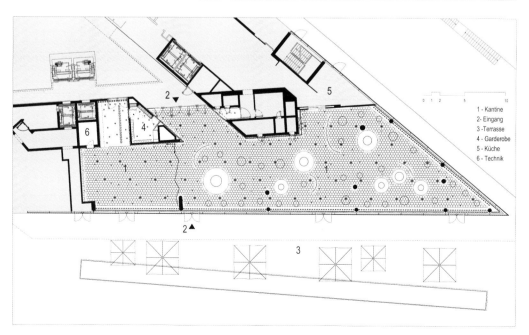

0 1 2   5   10

1 - Kantine
2 - Eingang
3 - Terrasse
4 - Garderobe
5 - Küche
6 - Technik

INDEX

and graphic design to video art and communication.

They look for the essence of things and express it in the most subtle way possible to enable end users to experience and interpret the space any way they desire.

BK projects include the development of residential buildings, private villas, civic centers as well as the interior design of restaurants, offices, hotels, bars, shops and residences.

The studio's work has received prizes and recognition from an international audience of magazines and institutions.

bkarc.com

Beige Design Ltd.
Hong Kong, China

Founded by Danny Chan, a talented and experienced interior designer with true passion in design, Beige Design Limited aims at creating stylish spaces with originality and a sense of elegance. With rich experiences in managing hotel design and commercial design projects, it offers an extensive design solutions ranging from hotel, clubhouse, show flat, residence, sales office, restaurant, retail shop, etc. Based in Hong Kong, its businesses cover Mainland China, Asia Pacific and overseas. Committed to provide creative and unique design space with exclusive and tailored design solutions, Beige excels in design quality, project management and art direction which empower their clients to strive for success and leading places in the market.

www.beige.com.hk

bluarch architecture + interiors + lighting
USA

Founded by Antonio Di Oronzo in 2004, bluarch architecture + interiors + lighting is an award-winning firm, a practice dedicated to design innovation and technical excellence providing complete services in master planning, architecture, interior design and lighting design. At bluarch, architecture is design of the space that shelters passion and creativity. It is a formal and logical endeavor that addresses layered human needs. It is a narrative of complex systems which offer beauty and efficiency through tension and decoration.

www.bluarch.com

Carsten Jörgensen
Switzerland/Denmark

Carsten Jörgensen holds an education as painter and graphic designer. After years as an art teacher in Copenhagen he started collaborating with the Danish coffee maker manufacturer Bodum in the early 70s. Until 2001 Jörgensen formed the entire product design of Bodum by designing the majority of the company's products and was its creative director for 25 years. Jörgensen's design has won international recognition since late 80s and is represented in major Museums around the world. Today Jörgensen is sharing his interest and activities between product design, design consultancy, lecturing and writing on art, design and architecture. Jörgensen has lived in Lucerne, Switzerland, since 1983.

COLLIDANIELARCHITETTO
Italy

Daniela Colli graduated from the Faculty of Architecture in Florence. She studied City and Guilds post-graduate course in London, obtaining a R.I.B.A qualification.

In Italy she worked in the fields of urban design and interior architecture with numerous architects, including Massimiliano Fuksas. She has been a consultant for Grandi Stazioni s.p.a. involved in the requalification of Italy's main railway stations and the relative urban infrastructure of Roma, Torino and Genova.

In 2009 she founded COLLIDANIELARCHITETTO, the practice works on a wide range of residential projects and commercial spaces such as shops, showrooms, spa, offices, cafes, restaurants and hotels.

www.collidaniela.com

Concrete Architectural Associates
the Netherlands

Founded in 1997, Concrete Architectural Associates is a multi-disciplinary creative office that builds identities, from urban planning to interior design, from architecture to product design.

According to Concrete, translating functionality and ease of use always depends on the given situation. Function has no definitive style. A museum needs a different design solution than a coffee bar, or a school or casino. And in outward appearance, they are nothing like each other.

Good design always starts with good analysis. A truly functional design must always be accompanied by an appropriate and stimulating concept. We live in a rapidly changing world with new lifestyles that demand radically different solutions than those that were offered one or two generations ago.

www.concreteamsterdam.nl/

Corvin Cristian
Romania

Corvin Cristian is a Bucharest based designer trained as architect. He worked most of his last 10 years as Art Director for movie sets, including many major builds. Designing period films as well as contemporary ones developed a versatility rarely happening in real-life projects. In between, Corvin designed trade fair pavilions, bars, restaurants and clubs, scenography for brand launches and other corporate events, retail design and offices. The conversion of a 1900 attic brought him the Award of the President of the Jury at the BAB (Bucharest Architecture Biennial).

www.corvincristian.com/

Curiosity Inc.
Japan

Curiosity Inc. is a design firm established by Gwenael Nicolas in Tokyo.

The portfolio includes interior design, package design, graphics and advertising. Gwenael Nicolas, the Frenchman with the British design education and his partner, Reiko Myamoto with her advertising background embrace the world with a foothold not only in Tokyo, but also in New York and Paris.

www.curiosity.jp

CUT Architectures
France

From public space to private space, from collective to individual housing, from artistic to functional, we work out the project through synthesis.

Our aim is to conceive projects in which plastic power and user comfort nourish themselves equally.

Our scope of work includes all scales and media, from urbanism to museum set design.

From long lasting architecture to ephemeral installations, our design results of experimentation and references in all the creativity domains without borders or hierarchy.

CUT Architectures is Benjamin Clarens and Yann Martin the office is based in Paris and was founded in 2008.

www.cut-architectures.com

Denis Kosutic
Austria

In Denis Kosutic's work, a new, anti-traditional perception of the role of architecture in the modern world manifests itself.

In his "prêt-à-porter-architecture", he masterfully translates the modern tendencies and trends from fashion and design into the language of everyday life and in doing so, he considers architecture as a subject of consumption, not a monument for eternity.

The process of planning also includes the elaboration of new strategies, the build-up image and corporate identity, the invention and establishment of codes that prompt people and brands to feel modern, unique and sought-after.

His office plans restaurants, clubs, shops as well as houses, apartments, hotel apartments and furniture, and cooperates with graphic designers, PR advisors and furniture producers

www.deniskosutic.com

Duarte Caldeira
Portugal

Founded by Portuguese architect Duarte Caldeira, the office focuses on architectural design at every scale, from urban planning to furniture. Its concept-based approach aims to create buildings, objects and spaces which engage their users and respond to their ambitions, cultures and contexts.

The ten-year-old practice is fuelled by talented and experienced architects who develop projects from the early sketches to on-site supervision. Every project involves a multidisciplinary professional team and external consultants who focus their knowledge, expertise and imagination on a fresh and innovative approach to design.

The office has a wide portfolio of work that includes public buildings, hotels, commercial and residential developments, as well as interior design and furniture.

www.duartecaldeira.com

elips design
UK

elips design is a design and research studio based in London, an RIBA chartered Practice. Even if the practice remains dedication to the realization of buildings, it also operates in areas beyond the traditional boundaries of architecture, including semiotics, renewable energy, technology, product design and graphic design. It has always been guided by a belief that the quality of our surroundings has a direct influence on the quality of our lives, whether that is in the workplace, at home or in the public realm. Allied to that is an acknowledgement that architecture is generated by the needs of people – both material and spiritual – and a concern for the physical context and the culture and climate of place. Equally, excellence of design and its successful execution are central to our approach. Environmental awareness is an integral part of the practice's culture as it evolves to meet the challenges of the next years.

www.elipsdesign.com

Elliott + Associates Architects
USA

Established in 1976, Elliott + Associates Architects is a full-service architectural firm of licensed architects, interior and graphic designers and support personnel. The firm has designed award-winning projects for corporate clients, various arts organizations, museums, and public spaces.

The design philosophy of the firm is shaped from the theory that a space reflects the unique personality of the owner, coupled with functionality. Elliott + Associates Architects creates special environments - architectural portraits - revealed as expressions of the client. Examining together who the client is, where he is going, and what he wants to accomplish. Defining the essence of who he is and his objectives enable the development of concepts to address the issues forming the basis of the portrait.

www.e-a-a.com

Expose ARCHITECTURE and DESIGN
Iran

The underlying idea behind all our design work is that well-designed buildings can enrich the quality of life of their users... We start by focusing on the basic building blocks of architecture:

Comfortable relationship with natural light and views,

Clear organization of space,

Comfortable proportions,

Energy efficiency,

A harmonious relationship between architectural space and the structural elements that define it.

www.exposearchitecture.com

facet studio
Australia

Our architectural journey starts from looking for the most suitable answer for given conditions such as budget, construction methodology, site regulatory restrictions, and natural environments.

Once we have figured out the design potential, we patiently polish that rough gemstone, injecting our passion and energy, until it shines with multifaceted radiance. This gem,

which acquired the eternal radiance, will be able to sustain its long-term value for our clients by skillfully distributing the clients' budgets. Finally these bright shining gems, through scattering them one after the other in the urban scape, we aim to on top of contributing to the wealth of individuals, also in a large perspective, contribute to the collective wealth of the society.

facetstudio.com.au

Femmes Regionales
Denmark

Femmes Regionales is a progressive design agency.

Since design and fashion is very much about all the unspoken and intuitive things: image, expression, the "je ne sais quoi", we always seem to add that important and special something you can't touch, in order to make things go from fair enough to fantastic!

We approach projects by finding a unique positioning and then embracing and combining different creative methods to make the big difference for your brand. By communicating innovative strategies and creative output for clients that dare to take new directions, we provide you with truly inspiring stories to tell.

Femmes Regionales is a state of mind, a vision for the future and a true love affair.

femmesregionales.com

Franziska Stromeyer, Frank Geiger
Germany

Franziska Stromeyer and Frank Geiger were 35 and 37 of age when they decided to throw themselves into cold water when opening up the Café "Suicide Sue" near Berlin's bustling Helmholtzplatz in 2009.

After years of working as a producer for commercials in Munich, Franziska decided to quit the movie - business and to finally work independently after having moved to Berlin in 2006 together with Frank, who worked as an airline - pilot at that time. It did not take much to convince him of starting a new adventure by opening the "Suicide Sue". He shifted from full- to part-time, but is still flying around when not calibrating the grinder at the café or tampering with Sue's three - group -espresso-machine.

The stylish interior, the good coffee and Franziska's warm smile finally made the "Suicide Sue" to a beloved place among Berlin's hipsters.

www.suicidesue.com

FreelandBuck
USA

FreelandBuck is an architectural design practice based in New York and Los Angeles affiliated with Yale and Woodbury Universities. Our office focuses on research and design, exploring the overlap between academia and practice.

www.freelandbuck.com

Honest Entertainment
UK

Honest Entertainment was founded in 2007 bringing together 20 years of combined experience from Tanya Clark and Heston Harper in film, theatre, food and set design. As a young, creative, dynamic team they have made their mark on the world of event and design by creating unforgettable environments.

Their novel approach and flare, immaculate attention to detail and unrivalled proficiency has led to Honest being recognized as leaders in their field with projects for the British Fashion Awards for the last 3 years, MTV European Music Awards 2009 & 2010, Hugo Boss, Vivienne Westwood, Gucci, Virgin, Ministry of Sound, Ikea, The British Heart Foundation and the Environmental Justice Foundation.

www.honestentertainment.co.uk

ILMIODESIGN
Spain

ILMIODESIGN is a new creative concept oriented to the design world in all its aspects. Into ILMIODESIGN we face, through a specific methodology, different processes of creation of a project: from architecture to interior design, through industrial and graphic design. Thanks to a great ability to adapt to the project and client's needs, ILMIODESIGN aims at obtaining results that are able to satisfy all phases of the project. From the beginning to the end, ILMIODESIGN puts together the client's requirements, with his tastes and desires, and the social and historical context of the project we are realizing. In this way hotel, commercial spaces and private houses originate.

www.ilmiodesign.com

Ippolito Fleitz Group
Germany

Ippolito Fleitz Group is a multidisciplinary, internationally operating design studio based in Stuttgart. We are identity architects. We work in unison with our clients to develop architecture, products and communication that are part of a whole and yet distinctive in their own right. This is how we define identity.

As architects of identity, we conceive and construct buildings, interiors and landscapes; we develop products and communication measures. We do not think in disciplines. We think in solutions. Solutions that help you become a purposeful part of a whole and yet distinctive in your own right.

www.ifgroup.org/

JM Architecture
Italy

JM Architecture, founded in 2005 by Jacopo Mascheroni and based in Milan, provides a range of architectural and design services to clients in Italy and abroad. The firm creates spaces where refined, pure, and timeless architectural lines meet with the most advanced technology to provide a graceful combination of exceptional aesthetic elegance, utility, and comfort. The works have earned national and international attention and have been published in print on four continents as well as widely published online. The dynamic output of the studio is driven by the collaboration of the firm's talented professionals who represent many nationalities and backgrounds and continuously strive to imbue the work with the ideals of simplicity, coherence, clarity and harmony.

www.jma.it

Jörn Fröhlich
Germany/Turkey

Jörn Fröhlich (born in Germany, 1970) is a freelance artist and designer covering theatre, fashion and retail design. He is based in Berlin/Germany and Izmir/Turkey, where he currently teaches visual merchandising, stage, costume, and multimedia design at Izmir University of Economics' Faculty of Fine Arts.

In 2010 he met Siddik Erdogan as a graduate student at Izmir University of Economics from where they started their collaboration on the Green Bistro.

jofro.com

Josep Ferrando
Spain

Josep Ferrando has been combining design, construction and academic activities. He has been teaching since 1998, some of the schools include: Escola Tècnica Superior d'Arquitectura de Barcelona (ETSAB), La Salle Engineering and Architecture School, University of Illinois at Chicago

(UIC), Istituto Europeo di Design (IED), and Escola de disseny i art (Eina). Additionally, he has been guest professor at: Hochschule für Technik Zürich (HSZT), Escola da Cidade in Sao Paulo, Universidade Positivo (UNICENP) in Curitiba and Universidade Federal do Paraná (UFPR). His work has been exhibited in several countries, amongst them the United States, Switzerland, Sweden, Norway and Portugal.

www.josepferrando.com

k-studio
Greece

Since 2002 k-studio has built up a varied portfolio of projects, believing that encouraging creative experimentation and fresh thinking leads to exciting architectural experiences on every scale and in every aspect of life.

www.k-studio.gr

Kamitov Project
Kazakhstan

Kamitov Project is a company specifies in commercial design projects, such as bars, restaurants, night clubs and hotels. It was founded in 2006.

www.kamitovproject.com

karhard architektur + design
Germany

karhard = thomas karsten + alexandra erhard, is founded in 2002 and based in Berlin.

karhard is an architecture and interior design firm. The office focuses mainly on the planning and the construction of clubs, restaurants & bars, shops and private housing.

Selected projects: 2003-2011 Berghain, Panorama Bar, Berlin; 2007 Deutsche Filmakademie Berlin; 2009 Tin Restaurant, Bar, Berlin; 2010 Tunnel Hair Berlin; 2011 Asphalt Club Berlin,

www.karhard.de

Luigi Rosselli Architects
Australia

With over 25 years of practice, Luigi Rosselli has built a reputation for quality individual, creative architecture covering a wide range of diverse applications including university facilities, adaptive re-use of existing structures, award winning new homes, alterations and additions to existing buildings and restaurant design. The work is not parochial or mainstream, not part of a school or trend.

It is never a one man show however. A team of enthusiastic young architects with fresh and innovative ideas is carefully nurtured to maturity. Luigi's 25 years in practice make the teamwork possible which sees innovative, high quality, award winning, inspiring homes built to the highest of standards. The team includes the best of landscape architects and interior designers who blend their ideas and those of the client into a coherent whole.

www.luigirosselli.com

Mas Arquitectura
Spain

With versatile, creative and innovative capacity, Marcos Samaniego Reimíndez (A Coruña, 1971) offers a refreshing vision of architecture. He is able to link natural resources with cultural heritage. His contact with European culture and design, during its formative stage in Barcelona, has accentuated his professional personality: details and the spaces have a particular goal, away from the impersonality.

His designs have been featured in international publications, as well as in newspapers and magazines. The combination of tradition and design is highlighted by experts, who consider Marcos Samaniego as one of the great promises of Spanish architecture.

www.mas.es

MSB Estudi taller d'arquitectura i disseny
Spain

MSB Estudi taller d'arquitectura i disseny was established in 2008, after a long and successful experience at RCR arquitectes, they have been collaborating with MIQUEL MERCE ARCHITECT since 2010.

MSB is a path, a story where the essence is creativity, where the work is the projects, the reflections and the experimentation. The projects are always connected to the world of architecture, interior, design and communication. The goal is to develop projects with personality and rigor, evolving concepts and discovering new elements that allow us to go further each time. MSB values pure forms, construction systems, and materials, attempting to reach a natural, tranquil, serene and essential state.

www.msbestuditaller.com

Mut-architecture
France

Mut-architecture is an architecture collective working in Paris, founded by John Mascaro & Léo Morand in 2008.

www.mut-architecture.com

Nuca Studio
Romania

A design studio based in Bucharest , Romania.

www.nuca-studio.ro

POINT.
Italy

POINT studio rises in 2012 from the common experiences shared from 2001 in the office formerly known as UAU. The office is based in Turin (Italy) but trends up overseas. Being a melting pot of different skills and attitudes, the studio turns its heterogeneity into a strength point. In the office, architects, visualizers and graphic designers work together to provide the clients with full quality projects, something near to a tailor made design. All the office's clients, from individual to the big company are both great challenge and big concern for all the staff. Its works are well known in Italy, and also in the Eastern countries, Europe and United States, having been published and awarded worldwide.

www.getthepoint.it

Projects of Imagination
Australia

POI is a multidisciplinary design consultancy that delivers a broad range of creative projects. Established by Dion Hall and Nick Cox in 2007, POI is today a studio with an increasingly visible national profile and client list. POI has extensive experience in the fields of brand development & interior design and consistently produces unique & culturally significant solutions across all creative platforms including built environments, installations, signage & product development, amongst others. POI is pioneering a new direction to design whereby a holistic process creates a more unique user-end experience. Purposely avoiding a stylized approach, each project brings a new artistic direction, a new metaphor or narrative that is specific to the design brief at hand. POI often collaborate with leading artisans in many fields and understand the importance of working closely with their clients, building meaningful relationships and delivering practical, commercially viable and original solutions.

www.projectsofimagination.com

Rashed Alfoudari
Kuwait

Rashed Alfoudari earned his Bachelor degree in Architecture in late 2010 from Kuwait University, Kuwait. He started his career as a freelancer, designing furniture pieces and small interior spaces for various clients. Having a passion for boutique restaurants & cuisine he teamed up with one of his colleagues and decided to start up their own Ubon. It's his first official project that was carried out from start to the end by him and his next step is to establish a design studio by partnering up with his colleagues.

ubonkw.com

rojkind arquitectos
Mexico

By addressing users' needs directly and seeing them as potential sources of inspiration and strength, rojkind arquitectos seeks new directions in architectural practice - evoking common identities through the exploration of uncharted geometries that address questions of space, function, technology, materials, structure, and construction methods related directly to geography, climate, and local urban experiences. By pursuing all projects that represent a particular design challenge, rojkind arquitectos has been able to develop a wide and ever-growing spectrum of designs initiatives, from the intimacies of small objects to the intricacies of large buildings and master plans.

www.rojkindarquitectos.com

Siddik Erdogan
Turkey

Ebubekir Siddik Erdogan (born in Turkey, 1987) is a freelance designer based in Izmir/Turkey. He graduated in 2009 from Izmir University of Economics in interior design. His design works are covering a wide range from architecture and interior design to digital animations with an expertise in 3D Visualization. In addition to his digital and conceptual design skills, he has profound knowledge of woodwork arts and crafts, which enables him to also manufacture complicated interior wood designs (see Green Bistro).

siddikerdogan.com

Slade Architecture
USA

We founded Slade Architecture in 2002, seeking to focus on architecture and design across different scales and program types. Our design approach is unique for each project but framed by a continued exploration of primary architectural concerns.

As architects and designers, we operate with intrinsic architectural interests: the relationship between the body and space, movement, scale, time, perception, materiality and its intersection with form. These form the basis of our continued architectural exploration.

Layered on this foundation, is an inventive investigation of the specific project context. Our broad definition of the project context considers any conditions affecting a specific project: program, sustainability, budget, operation, culture, site, technology, image/branding, etc.

Working at the intersection of these considerations, we create designs that are simultaneously functional and innovative.

sladearch.com

Studio SKLIM
Singapore

Studio SKLIM is an emerging design practice establishing its roots in the fields of furniture design, interiors, landscape, architecture and urbanism. Studio SKLIM was officially established in 2010.

The studio firmly believes that design opportunities are inherent, waiting to be unleashed or given a new perspective. The organization of "raw materials" not limited to the form of environmental data, existing typographical conditions, cultural peculiarities and technological limits form part of a platform from which our design process initiates these extractions. Analysis on our fast changing contemporary life demands a rethinking and reorganization of existing spatial parameters, thus making conceptual clarity and contemporary investigative research instrumental to the design process of our work. Our design ethos feeds on this rigor.

www.sklim.com

SWeeT co.,ltd
Japan

Takeshi Sano, designer and founder of SWeeT co.,ltd worked in the Production Department of Nissho Inter Life co.,ltd and the Development Uit of Global-Dining.Inc. He established SWeeT co.,ltd in 2003, focusing on interior to exterior design.

www.sweetdesign.jp

The Metrics
USA

We are a design consultancy dedicated to creating innovative social environments and hospitality experiences. We do architectural design, spatial installations, furniture and lighting design as well as identity and graphic projects and often collaborate across disciplines.

From designing hotels and restaurants to experimental temporary installations our work is always defined by a plot. As creating new experiences goes well beyond furniture, finishes and function, our design methodology is much like theater; always starting with a narrative that defines our process.

www.metricsdesigngroup.com

WHYDESIGN (Mauricio Arruda, Guto Requena, Tatiana Sakurai)
Brazil

WHYDESIGN is an architecture and design collective comprised by 3 architects and professors who use projects as actions that propose spaces and products to make us think, question and feel. With care for the transformation, needs and requirements of modern man, WHYDESIGN's projects try to use innovative materials and processes, whether for their formal, technological or environmental aspects. Commercial, residential, product and landscape projects are the foundation for beautiful stories to be told and experienced.

www.whydesignbr.blogspot.com

ACKNOWLEDGE-MENTS

We would like to give our special thanks to all the designers and owners for their kind permission to publish their works, and all the photographers who have generously granted us the right to use their images. Our thanks also go to the assistants, PR people and writers whose names do not appear on the credits. Without your support and assistance, we would not be able to share these amazing culinary design works with readers around the world.

Our publishing team includes Executive Editor Sasha Lo and Book Designer Feng Min, for whom we are sincerely grateful!